BASKETRY PLANTS USED BY WESTERN AMERICAN INDIANS

A study of traditional North American Indian basketry and plant materials used to create them with photos showing characteristics of the major plant materials used by basket makers.

by
Justin F. Farmer

Library of Congress Cataloging-in-Publication Data

Farmer, Justin F.

 Basketry plants used by western American Indians : a study of traditional North American Indian basketry and plant materials used to create them with photos showing characteristics of the major plant materials used by basket makers / by Justin F. Farmer. -- 1st ed.

   p. cm.

 ISBN 0-9761492-2-2

 1. Indian baskets--West (U.S.) 2. Basket making--West (U.S.) 3. Plants, Useful--West (U.S.) 4. Indians of North America--Material culture--West (U.S.) I. Title.

 E98.B3F37 2010

 746.41--dc22

                                   2010006978

Published by

The Justin Farmer Foundation
A Privately Endowed Charitable Fund
Mr. Joe Moreno, Foundation Chairman
1954 Evergreen Avenue
Fullerton. California 92835
(714) 256-1260

ABOUT THE AUTHOR:

Justin Farmer is an eighty-something year old collector and weaver of Indian baskets, with a special interest in southern California Indian arts. He has authored six books on Indian culture or basketry of southern California (plus one on how to hunt, pack out, and dress out a California black tail deer), and has lectured or given demonstrations of Indian basketry at twelve California universities. Mr. Farmer has conducted approximately thirty classes or demonstrations on creating southern California-style basketry, and is registered with the US Bureau of Indian Affairs (BIA) as a "Mission" (southern California) Indian. He is also registered with the State of California as a Professional Traffic Engineer, so he sometimes places a P.E. (rather than a PhD) after his name.

Disclaimer

As a professional engineer, he is well aware of the legal pitfalls associated with saying, as a professional person, that 2 x 2 = 4, and the lawsuits that inevitably follow. Therefore, he must emphasize that this treatise is not a gospel, and what is said is not chiseled in stone. It is intended to be a technical guide to native American plant materials used by many western North American Indians in their creation of basketry, and is oriented toward students, collectors, dealers, or simply devotees of Indian basketry. It is not intended to be a text on general botany of western North America, nor of the basketry of each North American Indian tribe.

Although a number of pages (chapter three) are devoted to basketry materials and weaving styles by many western US and Canadian tribes, it is not intended to be a detailed treatise on all baskets in all of western North America. Hopefully, however, it will aid persons in recognizing plants in a basket, thus assisting in the identification of a basket's tribal origin.

Acknowledgements

The author is indebted to Mr. Ryan Ahern, who assisted in preparation of photographs, figures, and tables in the manuscript.

TABLE OF CONTENTS

GLOSSARY

It has been said (by the author) that every racket has its own jargon. This certainly holds true regarding Indian basketry. Most of the terms used herein are more-or-less self-explanatory, but are defined below when there may be a question as to how the word, or term, was used in this narrative. In some cases the word, or phrase, is placed in quotation marks when the word is coined by the author and its meaning may be in question by the reader. In most cases the common name of a plant is capitalized to indicate that it is a Proper Name and should not be confused with the normal meaning of the word; e.g., Deer Grass, if not capitalized, would refer to an antlered animal and a weed it feeds on, which is not the meaning as used herein.

Customarily a glossary is placed in the back matter of a book. However, in this case, it is placed here, in the front matter, so that the reader is subjected to the word's usage prior to being exposed to it in the text.

Aniline dye: A modern commercial dye, such as RIT Dye, used primarily to color cloth or fabrics, but also used to dye a plant pattern material.

Anomaly: A discontinuity in a series of pattern motifs which appears to be unexplainable or unexpected.

Anthropomorph: A design motif depicting a human, either realistically or symbolically.

Awl: A sharply pointed device used to penetrate the coil foundation and open a hole for penetration of the "running end" of a weaver strand. In twining, an awl is used to compress the wefts into a uniform tightness or orientation.

Basal Red: The basal, or "earth" end of a Juncus reed containing a brick red color, used as a pattern material.

Bottle (jar): A basket consisting of a small flat base, wide flaring sides, a shoulder which is almost horizontal and in-sloping, and a narrow throat.

Cambium: The woody layer, immediately below the outer bark, which carries sap from the roots to the leaves.

Coiling: One of several basket manufacturing methods in which a foundation's core elements are wrapped by a weaver strand and spirals out and up to form the body of a basket; as contrasted to twining.

Crenulated: The serrated, or saw tooth-like edge of a plant's leaf.

Cross warp: Twining in which the warp (normally vertical elements) are at an angle, say at 45 degrees, not vertical. The wefts are, however, horizontal.

Diagonal twining: Plain or three-strand twining in which the weft crosses over two, rather than one, warp. This elongates the visible weft, which is then created in a stair step fashion so as to appear to be running diagonally up the basket surface.

Elder Brother: a.k.a. "The man in the maze". A design by some Arizona Indians which is a maze of somewhat joined concentric circles. The anthropomorphic figure represents a young man running to the home of his elder brother and is being pursued by a monster which will get lost in the maze.

Fag End: The butt, or last end of a weaver strand

to pass through the coil foundation. This is opposite the "running end", and is either bound under, like a half hitch, or is twisted (clipped) off after the weaver strand has dried.

Fancy basket: One in which the motifs are generally thin, tall, numerous, and well executed. Expertly created Washoe and some Mono Lake Paiute baskets are often so referred to.

Figure 4: A type of coiled basketry "start" in which the wide foundation materials form a cross. Common in Tohono O'odham baskets.

"Flint": A design motif similar to teeth on a saw, as used frequently in northern California.

Floral: A design motif representing a plant or flower, either realistically or symbolically.

Foundation: The inside, or core, of a coil in a coiled basket, consisting of either one, or more rods, or a bundle of slender plant elements, such as Deer Grass.

Fret: A horizontal series of interconnected "hooked" design motifs, similar to that used extensively in the Orient and in ancient Greece.

Full twist: An overlay form of pattern material in which the colored weft element is twisted through 180 degrees so the pattern appears on both the inside and outside surface of a twined basket.

Geometric: A design motif consisting of any of the geometric forms, such as a rectangle, triangle, circle, or linear element.

Grass   Another name for Deer Grass (*Muhlenbergia*).

Grasshopper stitch: A coiling method in which the weaver strand wraps the foundation upwards of six times before penetrating the underlying coil. This is also called an "interrupted" stitch, and is common in Mesoamerican baskets.

Imbricated: A style of coiling in which a separate pattern overlay element is placed over the wrapping material in a doubling-back, overlapping manner, resulting in what may resemble shingles on a roof. It is the imbricating element that develops pattern motifs.

"In-Between": A style of twining in which one whorl is plain two-strand twining and the next is a form of plaiting. Rarely used outside of British Columbia, Canada.

Ipai: (ee'pie): The tribal name often used for the northern Diegueno people of San Diego County, California.

Lattice weave: A twining style in which one of the wefts, a rather stout horizontal element, is wrapped by a much thinner weft on the outside surface of the basket. This style is used to add strength and rigidity.

"Mission":   When the word is capitalized and placed in quotation marks, it refers herein to a federally recognized tribe of Indians in southern California. The quotation marks distinguish an Indian tribe from a Spanish Catholic settlement.

Mortuary: A southern Yokuts style of basketry jar, allegedly used to store ashes from a cremation.

Mountain: Mountain and Valley describes a

horizontal pattern motif of short flat lines (mountain tops), then a vertical line (mountain's side), then a horizontal line (valley floor), then a vertical line to the top of the next mountain. This motif is sometimes referred to as a "cog" design.

Negative: A pattern created when colored weaver strands leave a blank area in the field in such a way as to create a pattern in the non-colored space. A classic example is the "T" in the Texaco service station logo, which is negative, in a positive red pattern.

"Non-work" side: That basket surface away from the weaver, where the awl emerges after penetrating the foundation. This side is usually less neat than is the "work" side.

Piki: A paper-thin form of bread made of corn meal by the Hopis.

Plaque: A flat circular wicker-style basket, often depicting a Katsina (Kachina), usually attributed to the 3rd mesa Hopis.

Plateau: That part of the western US which includes eastern Oregon, eastern Washington, a small part of Canada, parts of Idaho, and parts of Nevada.

Provenance: Description of a basket's origin, age, collector, tribe, and maker.

"Quail": Pattern motifs resembling a quail's top knot, usually thin, up-turned vertical stitches, which then turn horizontal, often attached to the side of a major pattern element.

Rhizome: A rather fleshy horizontal root from which plants sprout.

"Running end": That end of a weaver strand that is pointed and serves like a needle to first penetrate the coil foundation or to start the twining process.

Running pattern: Pattern motifs that are usually horizontal and joined, creating a chain-like connection. The motifs are usually a geometric form.

Scars: Locations on a weaver strand where a bud or twig left a depression or protrusion when the bark was removed.

Self: A basketry rim that is merely a continuation of the preceding weaving style; i.e., with no back stitches, herringbone, whip stitches, or braiding.

Shoot: That part of a tree or shrub that is long, slender, and used in creating a basket.

Skip stitch: A coiling style in which a noticeable gap is left between wrapping stitches; i.e., the wrapping stitches are not close together.

Skip-Stitch: A combination of plain two-strand and three-strand twining in which a textural pattern is created without use of color. Used primarily by the western (coastal) British Columbia weavers.

Snake: A pattern motif that consists of a series of boxed Xs that might be construed as a snake's back. The snake resemblance may be real or symbolic, with or without a head or tail.

"Start": The very beginning of a coiled basket, in which a wrapping material (weaver strand) in sewn about a foundation material. Three styles are identified herein; viz., 1) the "knot" type in which a hank of fiber is tied into an overhand knot and wrapped with a weaver strand like spokes on a wheel, 2) the "wad" type in which a bunch of fibers are squeezed into a wad and then penetrated repeatedly with a weaver strand, and 3) the "bent finger" type in which a straight bundle of fibers is wrapped for several inches and then bent back onto itself, like the fingers in a clinched fist.

"Sticks": Vertical members in an Indian basket or cradle board. Often called vertical warps.

Sunburned Willow: A pattern material used by some of the western Paiute weavers, created when the inner bark (phloem) is retained on the weaver strand and exposed to the sun, which turns the otherwise green phloem to a reddish brown color.

Terminal: The very last part of the last coil of a coiled basket, at the outer rim. Most terminals taper gently from full diameter to nothing, over one half to several inches.

Tipai (Tea-pie): The name often applied to the southern Diegueno people of San Diego County.

Three-rod: A coiled basket's foundation consisting of three whole rods, or shoots, of a material such as Willow, Juncus reeds, or any thin unsplit plant material.

"Throw-away": A basket hastily created in the field, usually of loose open twined Juncus, and intended for a single use, after which it is discarded.

"Trees": A pattern motif of a wide vertical element from which short horizontal elements extend.

Tribal Band: A subdivision of a larger group of

xviii Plants Used by Western American Indians

Indians, who are generally recognized as a tribe.

Twining: A basketry technique by which vertical elements (warps) are joined at the beginning, or "start", and then radiate out much like spokes in a wheel. Warps are joined together by horizontal wefts which are twisted about the warps.

Water bottle: A twined vessel often coated with pine pitch or asphalt, for holding water, like a canteen.

Warp: Vertical weaving elements in a twined basket, about which horizontal elements (wefts) are entwined.

Weaver strand: A longitudinal basketry element which is usually wrapped about a foundation material in a coiled basket. Occasionally a weft is referred to as a weaver strand.

Weft: A horizontal weaving element which wraps about the vertical (warp) elements in a twined basket.

"Work" side: That surface of a basket facing the weaver and the side of a coiled basket where the awl first penetrates the coil. It is almost always neater than is the other, or "non-work" side.

"Worms": Pattern motifs that resemble horizontal zig-zags. The horizontal units are one-half to one inch long. The horizontal motifs then drop down, and then continue horizontally a similar distance.

Zoomorphic: A design motif depicting an animal, bird, reptile, or insect, either realistic or symbolically.

Chapter 1

PLANTS USED BY WESTERN AMERICAN INDIANS

Introduction

Anybody who has any connection with American Indian basketry probably has a special (often secret) method by which he, or she, identifies the tribal origin of a specific art piece. Sometimes it is intuition, sometimes it's clairvoyance, and occasionally it's the voice of experience. However, just like those who have a fool proof way of beating the Las Vegas casinos, not all are 100% successful. In many cases, design motifs play a large role in tribal identification, while some "experts" consider the overall shape, such as a mortuary jar, as being diagnostic. Some (including the author) even consider the plant from which it was made, as being of paramount importance.

Your author does not claim to be an expert, nor even a clairvoyant, but he does know which end of a magnifier to look into. He also brags himself up that he can sometimes distinguish plant materials by using a 5x lens and some good light. Recognizing plant materials in an Indian basket, then, is what this overly long jumble of words is all about.

Therefore, the purpose of this dissertation is to display, via photographs and verbiage, what a specific basketry plant looks like while it is still growing, and then what it looks like after it is killed, skinned, butchered, trimmed, and sewn into a basket. The avowed intent is to show the basketry student, or devotee, or even the expert what, Willow looks like in contrast to peeled Red Bud, or Big Leaf Maple, or Hazel. Hopefully the reader, after digesting these pearls of wisdom, will be able to distinguish Red Bud, from dyed Woodwardia fern, or from basal red Juncus, or from "Sunburned Willow" and perhaps even recognize the minute differences between Devil's Claw and Bracken fern root.

After going to great lengths, and driving literally thousands of miles to obtain photos of about thirty-seven plant species, it occurred to the author that having a nodding acquaintanceship with plant materials, plus $1.65, will buy you a cup of coffee at some coffee houses. Plant recognition, then, is only the beginning. The student must also know what plants are associated with what tribes, under what circumstances. This may help to explain the thirty pages of narrative regarding fifty-seven western North American Indian tribes, and the plant materials used by each in their basket making.

The fact that only thirty-seven plant materials were selected for discussion certainly does not suggest that these are the only plants used by Indians of western North America. Indeed, there are almost as many plants that could have been used in basketry as there are lobbyists in Washington D.C. The specific thirty-seven plants were selected based upon their relative abundance in private and public collections at the beginning of the 21st century. True, other plant materials are found occasionally, but not as often as those discussed in the following chapters.

Regarding western North American Indian tribes, the fifty-seven tribes which are discussed in Chapter three represent those tribes in New Mexico, Arizona, Nevada, California, Oregon, the "Plateau," Washington, western Canada, and Alaska. However, only those who have contributed baskets that appear regularly, and in volume, in basketry collections at the time of this writing are included herein. To name every tribe in western North America would consume the remainder of the author's time in this valley of tears, and he has already sold part of that time to other endeavors.

Identifying an Indian Basket

Although this treatise is oriented toward the use of

specific plant materials in an Indian basket, it is recognized that knowledge of a plant material has little value unless it can be equated to a specific Indian tribe. Therefore, Chapter three contains a discussion regarding the major plant materials used by the fifty-seven tribes and their weaving characteristics. However, before plunging into specific tribal uses and characteristic, a few words are in order regarding the woes of being an Indian basket "expert."

Anyone who frequents the basketry circuit and brags himself up as a basketry expert will sooner-or-later be asked to identify someone else's baskets, and give an authoritative opinion on 1) who made the basket, 2) what tribe did she (or he) represent, 3) when was it made (how old is it), and 4) what is it worth? ... all for free ... Sure!

This author has traveled that route hundreds, if not thousands of times (please note that he also never exaggerates). Therefore, he has these comments regarding the above four questions:

Question #1 (Who made it?): It is almost impossible to tell, just looking at a basket, who made it, unless you like to massage the truth a bit, and there are heaps of experts who will massage the truth at least a tiny bit.

Question #2 (What tribe did she or he represent?): Sometimes, but not always, this is a piece of cake; that is, if you know your plant materials pretty well and have digested these pages thoroughly.

Question #3 (How old is it?): Again, this is almost impossible unless you really know baskets ... or ... you play awfully free and loose with your words. Occasionally there may be subtle clues as to its age, but usually it is almost impossible to estimate age of a basket or cradle by just looking at it. Besides, what particular advantage is there in having an old basket? Being old is an advantage in good wine, Social Security, and violins; but not necessarily in Indian baskets.

Question #4 (What is it worth?): If you get suckered into even considering this question, then you failed the course, miserably, and have even less sense than the financier that bought the ocean front property in Kansas ... for cash ... up front!

Now if you really want to put on a show for the folks, when this person (who wants all this free information) asks you these questions, just pull out your trusty 5X magnifier, walk over to where there is good light, ponder the matter seriously, scratch your nearly, or overly, bald forehead, wrinkle your brow, and finally state, very authoritatively ...Damned if I know!; i.e., if you really don't know. If you do have an idea as to its worth, beware! Telling a person their cherished, priceless, rare old Indian basket, which was acquired two days after your fore-bearer landed at Plymouth Rock, is worth $15.00 (high retail) is the best way in the world to create a mortal enemy. Trust me ...I'm an Indian ... would I lie?

By the time you have digested the myriad of words and photos that follow, you may be able to help out this gent who wants to pick your brain *pro bono*. If, on the other hand you try to impress someone, who isn't really worth impressing, and you give an answer to any or all of the above four questions, you get an "F" in the class. If you commit the unpardonable sin and give an estimate of the basket's value, you should really stop right here because you're probably well beyond redemption.

Anyway! ...

About methods of identifying baskets, your author has looked at literally thousands of Indian baskets, many in great detail. He has owned almost (or maybe more than) a thousand himself. He's spent thousands, perhaps even hundreds of thousands of dollars acquiring Indian basketry. He's spoken with hundreds of persons whom he believes to be knowledgeable, and has also picked the brains of experts in all walks of basket identification. His library is quite extensive and in the last five years he donated over 2,000 surplus books or titles on the subject from his personal library to various agencies or tribal bands. Based upon what he can glean, recognition of plant materials used in a basket is probably the safest and most reliable way to identify an Indian basket.

The reader should be advised that the impetus behind this treatise is plant material usage, not a detailed discussion of basketry styles, or how to construct basketry by every Indian tribe in western North America.

In the course of these ramblings, the reader should bear in mind that, notwithstanding the diatribe regarding "creativity", which is discussed later, basketry of a specific tribe in the 21st century may differ from that of the 20th century, which, in turn, may differ from the 19th century. It should also be recognized that summarizing basketry types and styles into a very short paragraph is almost certain to muddy up the water. For example, Willow root is used with respect to Sand Bar Willow but not with Arroyo or Black Willow. Information is scanty regarding use of Big Leaf Maple in a specific region, whereas it may have been used extensively by certain tribes in northern California.

Local names for plants are also a source of possible confusion; e.g., "Chaparral" is a Spanish word and is often used by botanists to describe a plant community of low growing shrubs, or a brushy hillside. However, to many central and northern California Indian basket makers, Chaparral refers to a specific plant (*Ceanothus cuneatus*), a.k.a. Buck Brush, or Deer Brush to the Indians and Wild Lilacs to some White Guys. Buck Brush is used extensively in creating baby cradles and occasionally in baskets.

Another commonly used term, Bull Pine, is used in some places to describe one species of pine (*Pinus spp.*), whereas the same term used in another region refers to an entirely different tree. Spruce is a botanical name used to describe a given family of trees. However, in some parts of the west, a Spruce is a tree from a different family altogether. The same can be said of the word Cedar, or Fir. If the truth were to be known, most Cedars aren't Cedars at all, and many Firs aren't really firs. However, when a term is used in reference to a basket, most people know what is meant and not what is said.

The term "Conifer root" is used quite extensively in northern California and in some parts of the Pacific Northwest. There are numerous references in the literature to the use of Conifer root as a weaver strand. However, there seems to be little agreement as to which of the conifers is being referred to. To a lumber jack, the term conifer means a tree that bears a cone, such as a pine or cedar, or fir. However, when the term Conifer root is used to describe a specific basketry material, no such categorization is possible because many people (including this author) cannot tell the root of one conifer from another.

About Tradition

Before we launch this tirade about basketry materials, let's say a few words about tradition. In the humble opinion of the author, tradition is basically what makes the world go around. If we did not have a tradition of applying the brakes of our cars to make them stop, or opening our mouth just before we eat, we would not be here enjoying Indian basketry.

To most Indian basket makers, tradition was a hard and fast rule. If Indian basket weavers did not adhere very strictly to tradition, we would know absolutely nothing about Indian basketry, or culture, or ethnography, or anything else about the old ones; i.e., nothing, nada, zero, zip, nil. If you, as a basketry novice, were to ask a basketry expert what it is that makes a certain basket characteristically Cahuilla, or Pomo, or Hupa, 99 times out of every 88, that expert will tell you that the Cahuilla, or Pomo, or Hupa people followed strict traditional rules, and that a weaver from that tribe created baskets, or cradles, almost exactly the way her mother did, and her mother's mother did before her. If a serious student takes the time to study even a modicum about characteristics of a given tribe, there isn't any great secret to identifying basketry of that tribe, because each weaver followed century old traditions and did not vary more than a half a centimeter from the use of traditional materials or techniques of her (or his) tribe.

Several years ago, The Justin Farmer Foundation was privileged to have financially assisted a lady, Susan Lobo, in filming items from the "Malaspina Collection" in a museum in Madrid, Spain. Malaspina was a Spanish sea captain who collected Indian arts and cultural items along the Pacific Coast of the new world circa 1792; that is, before there was any appreciable contact with Europeans, who started arriving in California in 1769. In fact some of the locations Malaspina collected from had never been visited before by a non-Indian. Some of the Malaspina baskets were well used in 1792 and originated in a region never before occupied by Europeans, which means they reflect a snap shot of what basketry materials and characteristics were in use prior to any outside influence. Of the fourteen (+/-) Chumash baskets in that Malaspina collection, there is virtually no difference between the pre-contact (pre 1769) basketry and those being made 240 years later. What does this mean? It speaks to the influence of tradition and how it enables a poor 21st century country boy, like me, to feel confident in identifying a Chumash basket created 240 years ago. It also shows that weaving styles and materials have not materially changed over the last two (+) centuries. Were it not for tradition in basket making, we would have very little knowledge of the culture and history of Indians 240 years ago, and if we don't know about their history, we don't know diddly today about Indian baskets.

Teaching the Art Form

Regarding Indian basket makers in the *Once Upon a Time* years, young ladies were generally taught basketry art by their 1) grandmother, or 2) their aunt, or 3) their mother, or 4) some kindly old spinster or widow who had no daughter of her own. If the young weaver was a boy, he was generally taught by his grandmother. The young weaver was taught about plant materials; i.e., where they grew, when they were harvested, harvesting etiquette, material aging/curing, preparation, dying, trimming, etc. Next she (or he) was instructed in how the elders made a basket, what patterns could or could not be used, what pattern motifs were owned by the family, or another family, and finally what taboos were in effect. A young weaver was taught pride in being a member of the tribal family, and tried very hard to make the family proud. The last thing in the world a weaver would do is break tradition, which was sure to bring shame down on the family and weaver, and boy... shame to an Indian is almost, but not quite, as bad as standing in line at the welfare office on Monday morning.

Unfortunately basket making went into a slump in the early-middle 20th century, and, although many weavers continued in northern California and the Pacific Northwest, basket making almost died out in central and southern California and in the Southwest. Fortunately, the art form was rescued in the late 20th century and is now a thriving cottage industry. However, the grandmother-granddaughter relationship almost died out in the middle 20th century.

Moving right along ...!

Creativity

One of the author's pet peeves is what he refers to as "creativity," sometimes laughingly called "artistic license." Our 21st century, Anglo-Saxon-American culture is saturated with creativity; we are plagued by creativity. Creativity hounds us at every turn of the internet. Our culture literally drivels with creativity. We have too damn much creativity. Our art world has so much creativity that we have advanced to a point where we have no recognizable art form at all; again... nothings, nada, nil, zero, zip. Our art works of January are trashed and end up on the bargain rack in front of Borders Books store in July. Our flat graphic art is totally unrecognizable a week after it comes off the press, unless the artist signs it in 3/4" tall capital letters in the lower right hand corner. Our Monday morning designer clothing has so much creativity that it is out of style before it hits the 18 hour sale next Saturday. A few years ago the race was on to see how much skin, from the big toe to the chin, could be covered up by a lady's "granny outfit". Today, with creativity in clothing design, both visible and next to visible, the race is on to see how much skin can be exposed from the belly button... both ways.

Thus far the words of the author!

Evolution of Our Plant Knowledge

Ever since book authors came down from the trees and started writing about Indian baskets, they (we!) have expounded upon the various plant materials and how they were used in Indian baskets. The only trouble is, most of these learned book writers (us) knew less about plant materials than did the guy they hired to saddle up their riding ostrich for a ride across the Himalayas. In the not-so-distant past, references were frequently made using esoteric, pseudo-scientific terms, such as ... reeds, rushes, twigs, switches, limbs, roots, grass, etc., all of which smack of a paucity of knowledge of the subject about which they were writing. Early basket collectors were only one cut above (or maybe below) book authors. They were often blatantly wrong about plant materials in baskets. It was not until the early 1970's that people like the late Bill Cain and Dr. Chris Moser, and Eva Slater, and Jerry Kasparek, and Craig Bates, and Brian Bibby started to really look at baskets with a 5X magnifier. What did they find? You guessed it... most of the previous descriptions of basketry materials were woefully inadequate and the book had to be completely rewritten; and that's exactly what Chris Moser and Craig Bates and Brian Bibby did.

During the middle-late 1970s the late Dr. Chris Moser, then Curator of Anthropology at the Riverside Metropolitan Museum in Riverside, invited a small group of persons to visit his museum and take a fresh new look at the 3,000 (+/-) baskets down in the catacombs. He was specifically interested in plant materials and construction techniques. That group, consisting of Art Silva, Jerry Kasparek, Eva Slater, Justin Farmer, and the late Bill Cain, met monthly for more than a year. They looked at almost every single basket in the collection and offered a variety of detailed opinions. Needless to say, not all opinions were unanimous but they did represent the collective knowledge of people who at least knew what end of a magnifier to look into. It is pretty safe to say that many of the museum's accession documents were found to be either questionable, or downright incorrect, and it was the collective opinion of this group that no documentation is often better than spurious documentation.

Starting in 1981 Dr. Moser mounted a series of exhibits of Indian baskets from the Riverside Municipal (now Metropolitan) Museum's collection. The first consisted of a display of nearly 500 southern California baskets at five separate but simultaneous venues. The event was entitled *Rods, Bundles, and Stitches,* and its catalogue very quickly became The Bible regarding southern California Indian baskets, specifically regarding plant materials. Within a few years Dr. Moser mounted the second of his California basket exhibits, featuring items from central California, including a fine catalogue entitled *Native American Basketry of Central California.* This second catalogue was followed closely by his third exhibit entitled *American Indian Basketry of Northern California,* which, in turn, was followed by his fourth exhibit/catalogue entitled *Native American Basketry of Southern California.*

These four major exhibits and catalogues were soon followed by smaller but no less detailed exhibits of baskets by the 1) Hopi, 2) Apache, and 3) Pacific Northwest, all from the museum's collection. Each exhibit featured details on plant materials used in the baskets under display. Unfortunately time and expenses precluded a major catalogue on these latter events.

Then on the seventh day he (Dr. Moser) rested.

Publication of the Dr. Moser catalogues apparently sparked wide-spread interest in basketry plant materials and emphasized the fact that perhaps the most important clue to identifying an Indian basket is the plant materials used in its construction. It might be said that the efforts of Dr. Moser's emphasis on plant materials in identifying tribal origins is the impetus behind this current thesis.

Plant Usage as We Know It Today

Basketry nuts of the early 21st century are a lot more sophisticated (less nutty) than we were in the 1970s. Rather than make wild guesses as to what a plant material might be, and thus risk a spurious identification of a basket, we now consult specialists who have studied these plants, sometimes almost to a fault. We now have back room guys who can identify a specific plant even if it is 100 years old and in a sadly mistreated condition.

The reader will note that numerous caustic references are made throughout this narrative regarding the need for, and use of, a good; i.e., a $4.98 (plus tax) magnifier. Inasmuch as recognition of plant materials is deemed (by the author) to be essential to an identification of baskets, it is imperative that the basketry student be able to look into the very bowels of a weaver strand, as it may be found in an Indian basket. This is almost impossible without the use of a good magnifier and the knowledge of how to use it. That is because it is virtually impossible to tell many of the plant materials apart without the aid of a good magnifier. For example, in a reasonably old basket, distinguishing between Willow and peeled Red Bud, or Big Leaf Maple is very difficult. Magnification should be of the order of 5X but not over 8X-10X. Once a glass is above about 7X, its focus and depth of field becomes a problem and what you gain in magnification is lost in focus and over-magnification. A number of the author's close friends claim to be basketry authorities but do not even own a magnifier. This gives some people serious cause to question their actual knowledge.

In many, if not most cases, identifying a basketry plant is not all that mystifying. Unfortunately, many collectors, and some dealers, are unwilling to take the time, or spend the effort, to learn very much about these materials. It is the sad experience of your author that some High Rollers, who are willing to purchase a $300,000.00 basket, and pay in cash (plus an 18 percent buyer's premium), will cringe when asked to pay $4.98 (plus tax) for even a fair magnifier. Nor do many of these High Rollers know which end of the magnifier to look through even if they did blow the $4.98 (plus tax). That's probably because they don't know what kind of a plant they are looking at even if they did spend the $4.98 (plus tax).

In a nutshell, is all about identifying plant material used by a weaver as she (or he) created a basketry art piece.

Chapter 2

PLANTS CONSIDERED AS BASKETRY MATERIALS

Listed on the following pages are a few of the more commonly used plants which are (were) used by western American Indians to create basketry. The list is by no means all-inclusive, and certainly the reader can name dozens of others that are, or were, used occasionally. It is recognized that Indians of western North America have a cornucopia of plants that could be, and may have been, used to create baskets, either by coiling, twining, twilling, plaiting, or just plain braiding. In an earlier paragraph it was stated that tradition dictated that only specific plants were to be used by a given tribe and that only traditional gathering, curing, preparation and weaving techniques were acceptable.

The plants discussed herein are all believed to be indigenous. Indigenous is a sage old Indian word meaning it was not brought over here when the Olduvai gorge outcasts left sunny South Africa and trouped over the one mile thick X 5,000 mile long Siberian ice pack 13,276 years ago. For our purposes herein, indigenous plants are defined as those used by American Indians prior to contact with those newly arrived folks in the brown wool night gown and an old cotton-rope belt. After arrival of these strangers, exotic plants found their way into the Indian's range land where they may have been eaten, used for medical purpose, or even made into arrows. Exotic, as used herein, has nothing to do with expressive dancing: it is the opposite of indigenous. In most cases, only indigenous plants were used in creating basketry art by early Indian basket makers.

A study of plant communities of western North America

suggests that some plants, which were used in one geographic area, may also have flourished in another region. However, tradition dictated that they could not be utilized in the second area; e.g., Red Bud is native to much of California, but Red Bud was never utilized in southern California basketry. Likewise Deer Grass (*Muhlenbergia rigins*) is so wide spread that it may even have grown on Mars. However it was (is) used only in southern and central California. Its basketry use on Mars is still under study by NASA. At least one species or variety of *Juncus* is reported to be native to almost every county in California and most states in the western US. Yet *Juncus* was used for basketry only in southern California, and by the Panamint people near Death Valley, the Chemehuevi people near the Colorado River, and the Moapa Paiutes of central Nevada.

Listed below are plants defined herein as Indian basketry materials in the western US, Alaska, and Canada. The first column in that list is the common name while those in parentheses are botanical names. Where several different species or varieties of a given plant were used, the term *spp.* is listed. The term *spp.* is also used when the exact species is unknown.

A word or two regarding plant common names: some botanical names change almost as fast as do prices on a gallon of gasoline. For example, Incense Cedar was known for years as *Librocedrus*, but is now listed in Hickman's *Jepson Manual* and Moerman's *Native American Ethnobotany* as *Calocedrus*. At one time Deer Grass was called *Epicampis* but is now called *Muhlenbergia*. Poison Oak used to be a member of the Sumac family (*Rhus diversiloba*) and half brother to Sour Berry, a.k.a. Basket Weed, but is now *Toxicodendron diversilobum*. Referring to *Pinus sabiniana as* "Digger Pine" is now almost as popular as using the "N" word. In years past, many stupid people referred to an Indian lady as a Squaw, and the plant Sumac as "Squaw Bush." The word "Squaw" is a French corruption of an Indian word which refers to a lady's private anatomy and is far from being complimentary when applied to an Indian lady. To use that term today really displays a person's gross ignorance (ignorance is a sage old Indian word meaning stupid in English.) Therefore, recognizing the fluidity of botanical and Indian names, the reader is asked not be too harsh when an obsolete term, or one somewhat foreign to a specific reader, is used herein.

Common name   (botanical name)

Common name	(botanical name)
Alder,	*Alnus spp.*
Bear Grass,	*Nolina microcarpa* (Arizona and the Southwest)
Bear Grass,	*Xerophyllum tenax* (California and Pacific Northwest)
Bracken fern,	*Pteridium spp.* (root only)
Bulrush root,	*Scirpus spp.* (a.k.a. Tule Root)
Cattail,	*Typha latifolia*
Cedar bark/root,	*Calocedrus spp.* (Incense Cedar) *Chamaecyparis lawsoniana* (Port Orford Cedar) *Thuja plicata* (Western Red Cedar), etc
Chaparral,	*Ceanothus spp.* (a.k.a. Buck or Deer Brush, Wild Lilac, or "Wait-a-Bit")
Choke Cherry,	*Prunus virginiana*
Conifer root,	*Pinus spp.* [Ponderosa, "Sidehill" (Gray), "Bull", or Sugar Pine] *Pseudosuga spp.* (Douglas Fir) *Picea spp.* (Spruce), etc.
Cottonwood,	*Populus fremontii*
Deer Grass,	*Muhlenbergia rigins* (a.k.a. Clump or Bunch Grass)
Devil's Claw,	*Martynia spp.*
Dogwood,	*Cornus spp.* (Creek Dogwood)
Grape,	*Vitis californica*
Grape root	*Vitis californica* (root only)

Hazel,	*Corylus rostrata*
Juncus,	*Juncus textilis* (Wire Grass)
Maidenhair fern	*Adiatum pedatum* (Five Finger Fern)
Maple,	*Acer macrophylum* (Big Leaf Maple)
Milk Weed,	*Asclepia spp.* (fiber only)
Nettle,	*Urtica spp.* (fiber only)
Palm leaf,	*Washingtonia filifera*
Rabbit Bush,	*Chrysothamus nauseous* (Rubber Bush)
Red Bud,	*Ceris occidentalis*
Sedge,	*Carex spp.* (a.k.a. White Root)
Spruce root,	*Picea spp.*
Sumac,	*Rhus trilobata* (Sour Berry, Basket Weed)
Tule,	*Scirpus spp.*
Willow shoots,	*Salix spp.* (any of several species/ varieties)
Willow Root,	*Salix spp.* (Sand Bar or Gray Willow)
Woodwardia,	*Woodwardia chamisoi* (Giant Chain fern)
Yucca (fiber),	*Yucca whipplei* (Our Lord's Candle)
Yucca (leaves),	*Yucca elata* (Soap Tree)
Yucca (root),	*Yucca brevifolia* (Joshua Tree) *Yucca schidigera* (Mojave Yucca) *Yucca bacata* (Banana Yucca)

Where there is a difference between Jepson's 1923 *Manual of Flowering Plants of California*, Hickman's revised *Jepson Manual*, and Moerman's 1998 *Native American Ethnobotany*, or some other reputable authority, the author kind of waltzed around the issue by simply listing *spp.* The above list includes some plants which yield cordage, rather than what is normally considered a weaver strand. These are included because they are often either associated with, or are actually a part of, the basket. Conspicuous by its absence is a discussion of Indian Hemp (Dogbane, or *Apocynum spp.*). Dogbane was (is) probably the most widely used fiber material in most of western North America. It is an extremely strong, soft, readily available plant material used for all forms of cordage. Some varieties produce fibers almost as soft as silk. However, it was rarely, if ever, used in creating basketry in our study area. An exception might be where a carrying strap or wrapping fiber was used, or in some Plateau Sally Bags.

Also conspicuous by its lack of discussion are beads, either glass, stone, bone, or shell. Use of beads, and even sometimes rattlesnake rattles on a basket or cradle, is often an important feature that should not be overlooked. However, like beads or cloth, such rattles are not considered as a plant material herein. The same can be said of commercial cloth or yarn. Use of bird feathers, either whole or only the quill, is another feature of many California baskets. The Pomo weavers often covered a portion, or all, of a weaving with gaily colored feathers like mallard duck, woodpecker scalps, meadow lark breast, pheasants, etc. A number of weavers used bird feather quills in their patterns; e.g., Pomo, Hat Creek, and Panamints. Although they may have been used occasionally, or even frequently, they are not considered to be a plant material so are not discussed in any detail herein.

Chapter 3

MATERIALS USED BY SPECIFIC TRIBES

Tribes of California

Listed herein are a few of the western US Indian tribes and some of their basketry characteristics. Not all of the western US Indian people are represented because there isn't that much ink in my printer cartridge to print them all, and besides, cartridge ink is almost as expensive as gasoline, which, in turn, is considerably less expensive, per gallon, than is plain bottled drinking water.

The tribal names used herein are those in common use by basketry nuts and may not necessarily be those used by the people themselves. An attempt was also made to discuss the several weaving styles in use by each listed group. In some cases, a notation is made that a tribe rarely made a coiled or twined basket. The word "rarely" is used rather than "never" because never is an awful long time and presumes something that is never certain. Data in this chapter is necessarily abbreviated because the primary theme of this entire dissertation is oriented toward recognition of specific plants, not a detailed discussion of each tribe's weaving techniques.

Note that in the verbiage which follow, the term tribe, or tribelet, or band is often associated with, but does not imply, a tribe as it is commonly thought of; such as the Comanche tribe, or the Sioux, or Cheyenne, or Haida tribes. Inasmuch as California and most Pacific Northwest people hadn't invented the concept of a tribe, the term is used herein very loosely to designate an Indian group.

A few words might be in order at this point regarding the sequence in which the tribes are arrayed below. The first to be discussed, just by chance, happens to be in southern California with the Diegueno people, who, coincidentally, just happen to be the tribe to which the author traces his lineage. The sequence then progresses north thru coastal California to about the Oregon Border, then easterly to California's northeastern corner, then southerly along the Sierra Nevada eastern front, including western Nevada, down to Death Valley, then into Arizona and New Mexico, working west to east. After running out of Arizona and New Mexico tribes, the text then jumps to southwestern Oregon and works its way north through Oregon. It then jumps again to the "Plateau"; i.e., that area of eastern Oregon, eastern Washington, and western Idaho, then works its way westerly along the Columbia River region to southwestern Washington, then north into British Columbia, and Alaska. Beyond Alaska, the text ends, otherwise the reader might fall over the top. Inasmuch as basketry from the Pacific northwest is somewhat limited, selection of tribes in that region is almost as random as a teenager's choice of hair styles.

This chapter discusses, very briefly, each of the 57 tribes' weaving materials and styles. The narrative is necessarily abbreviated, and the authors of the Chicago Manual of Style would be horrified if they were to read the next 32 (+/-) pages; i.e., the abbreviations, coined terms, and incomplete sentences. You, the reader, however, are more forgiving and hopefully will understand what information is being conveyed, in as few words as necessary. If it can be said in ten words, why use 20!

Please bear in mind that this treatise is not intended as an all-encompassing description of western North American basketry. It is limited to specific plants in basketry of only the more well-represented tribes.

Style	Material-Patterns-Characteristics

Diegueno ("Mission")

Coiling   Clockwise.

Juncus, Sumac, Deer Grass (foundation), Yucca fiber ("starts"), Devil's Claw very rare; i.e., in the very southeastern portion of San Diego County only. Basal red Juncus and Sumac very common, black Juncus sparingly. Fag ends bound under, bottoms rarely flat, usually convex.

Patterns: Mostly geometrics in basal red Juncus, minimal dyed black Juncus. Few zoomorphs or floral motifs. Mostly isolated geometric motifs.

Twining   Rare. If present, open twined bowls or tightly twined hats of whole Juncus warps and wefts. Patterns rare.

Cupeno * ("Mission")

Coiling   Clockwise.

Juncus, Sumac, Deer Grass (foundation), Yucca ("starts"). Stitch count often quite high. Basal red and black Juncus common, Sumac used sparingly. Fag ends bound under.

Patterns: Mostly in black Juncus or negative in Sumac, slightly busy resembling Cahuilla-Diegueno hybrid. More zoomorphs (animals) than Diegueno, but mostly isolated geometrics, similar to the Ipai (Northern Diegueno).

Twining   Rare. If present, will be open twined "throw away" utility ware with whole Juncus warps and wefts.

(*) The Cupeno referred to here are those who formerly lived near Warner's Hot Springs in northeastern San Diego County before they were evicted and relocated to Pala circa 1903.

Luiseno ("Mission")

Coiling   Clockwise.

Juncus, Sumac, foundation of Deer Grass. Yucca fiber (knot) or Deer Grass (wad) "starts". Split Juncus foundation not uncommon. Fag ends bound under. Bases often convex. Sumac is normally the stitching material, minimal basal red Juncus, motifs mostly in black Juncus.

Patterns: Usually austere, of isolated geometric motifs. Black horizontal bands common, almost diagnostic, often encompassing a pattern of connected or multiple geometrics. Isolated vertical or spiraling motifs are common. Zoomorphs or floral motifs rare.

Twining   Rare.

Juaneno ("Mission")

Coiling   Clockwise.

Juncus, Sumac, foundation of Deer Grass, Yucca fiber knot or Deer Grass "starts". Fag ends bound under.

Patterns: Similar to Luiseno; i.e., austere and almost always in black Juncus with minimal basal red. Black bands are rare and geometric motifs are relatively few, isolated, and usually stacked vertically.

Twining   Rare.

Note: Although there are a number of baskets attributed to Juaneno weavers, the number of those with good provenance is extremely rare, numbering perhaps less than several dozen, in the entire world. Therefore, the characteristics noted herein are based upon a minimal amount of analyses of baskets with good provenance.

Cahuilla ("Mission")

Coiling   Clockwise.

Juncus, Sumac, Palm Leaf (*Washingtonia filifera*), foundation of Deer Grass, Yucca fiber "starts". Fag ends are either clipped, bound under, or both. Bases are almost always flat.

Patterns: "Busy", extensive bold black Juncus, sometimes almost garish. Many zoomorphs, anthropomorphs. Floral motifs and geometric elements usually isolated but occasionally joined, including lightning, whirlwind, spirals, or even solid blocks of color. Overall patterns often tell a story or include names or initials.

Twining   Rare, possibly "throw away" similar to the Dieguenos, but few are extant.

Note: There are three major divisions of the Cahuilla; i.e., Mountain, Pass, and Desert. Each differs in their basketry but all are similar overall. Desert Cahuilla baskets often have clipped fag ends and Palm leaf stitching material. Pass Cahuilla weavers often use the whirlwind pattern, while Mountain Cahuillas use much more basal red Juncus.

Serrano ("Mission")
Coiling   Clockwise.

Juncus, Sumac, Yucca root (Joshua Tree or Mohave Yucca), foundation of Deer Grass, Yucca fiber "starts". Fag ends mostly bound under but occasionally clipped. Bottoms are usually flat.

Patterns: Similar to both the Mountain Cahuilla and Northern Diegueno (Ipai); i.e., much red, but also much black Juncus. Motifs busier than those of the Ipai. Arrowhead motif is almost a signature from arrowhead on the mountainside above San Bernardino. Use of maroon/red Yucca root for pattern is diagnostic.

Twining Rare.

Chemehuevi (*)
Coiling   Clockwise.

Juncus, Sumac, Willow, Devil's Claw, Yucca root, Deer Grass (foundation). Cottonwood foundation rare. Willow over three-rod Willow common. Fag ends occasionally bound under, mostly clipped. Yucca fibers often as "starts".

Patterns: If the basket originated in the Coachella Valley it closely resembles the Desert Cahuilla, with a Deer Grass foundation. If from the Colorado River region there will almost always be a black rim of Devil's Claw and relatively few isolated zoomorphs or geometrics of black on Willow. Willow is a common stitching and foundation material.

(*) At one time Chemehuevi people lived in the Coachella Valley as well as in the High Desert of San Bernardino

County and near Victorville. Basketry from these areas closely resembles that of the Desert Cahuilla or Serrano. Chemehuevi people currently live in the Colorado River region and their basketry is now more akin to the Southwest people of Arizona. However, those baskets created in the Coachella Valley region are often hard to distinguish from those of the Cahuilla or Serrano.

Gabrielino ("Mission")

Coiling   Clockwise.

Juncus, Sumac, foundation of split or 3 whole-rod   Juncus, some Deer Grass (foundation). Yucca fiber or   split Juncus ("starts"), fag ends clipped or bound under.

Patterns: usually austere albeit similar to Chumash if in close proximity. In the Los Angeles basin, patterns are mostly horizontal bands of weakly dyed black or pale red Juncus. Geometric motifs are rare, zoomorphs, anthropomorphs or floral motifs almost never, some "worms" similar to the Chumash.

Twining   Rare, except in the northern frontier where they may resemble Chumash ware.

Note: Gabrielino baskets are exceedingly rare, and those with good provenance are believed, by the author, to number in the dozens, rather than the thousands like the Cahuillas or Dieguenos. Characteristics listed here are believed, by the author, to be realistic but are based upon a limited number of specimens.

Chumash

Coiling   Clockwise.

Juncus, Sumac, whole 3-rod Juncus foundation, Deer Grass foundation occasionally. Fag ends mostly clipped, rarely bound under.

Patterns: May be quite intricate. The "classic" pattern may contain a "primary band," "body filler," a "basal band", and often "rim ticking." Some, however, are similar to Luiseno; i.e., isolated black Juncus geometrics but with a 3-rod Juncus foundation.

Twining   Plain twining for water bottles and some utility vessels which are usually non-rigid. Open twining rare. Bottles are often coated with asphalt (tar). Twining skills are not comparable to those in northern California.

Costanoan

Because of the rarity of these baskets, little can be said of their typical characteristics.

Salinan

Coiling   Clockwise.
Sedge, Bracken fern root, glass beads, Horsetail fern root. Coiled or twined baskets are quite rare and few are attributed to Salinan. There are so few of these baskets with good provenance that it is almost impossible to develop a typical case.

Valley Yokuts

Coiling   Clockwise.
Sedge, Bracken fern root, Willow, Red Bud, Cottonwood (rare), foundation of Deer Grass. Feathers or wool not uncommon. Fag ends clipped. "Mortuary jars" with flat shoulders common, many deep basin bowls, mostly of Sedge root and Red Bud or Bracken fern root.

Patterns: Horizontal bands of joined "x's" (a.k.a. snake pattern), anthropomorphs holding hands ("friendship"), geometrics, quail top knots, zig zags, vertical motifs (trees) quite common.

Twining   Sedge, whole or split Red Bud, Willow or Cottonwood warps. Tule mats for receiving cradles.

Tubatulabal

Coiling   Clockwise.
Sedge, Willow, Red Bud, Bracken fern root, Yucca root, Devil's Claw, possibly Bulrush (Tule) root. Cloth or feathers rare. Foundation of Deer Grass or Willow.   Fag ends clipped.

Patterns: Similar to Foothill Yokuts, or Kawaiisu or Panamint. Horizontally joined (running) diamonds, Vees, stacked   triangles, spiraling stair steps. Hard to distinguish from neighboring tribes.

Twining   Rare, Sedge, Red Bud and Willow warps.

Kitanemuk

Although a number of baskets are attributed to the Kitanemuk people, few have good provenance, other than the owner's say-so. Therefore, little is known, positively, about their characteristics. If their basketry is coiled, it probably coils clockwise, based upon the geographic spread of right versus left handed coiling. Discussions with what the author considers reliable authorities, suggests that Kitanemuk basketry is similar to that of the Foothill Yokuts or Tubatulabals. Because they are located in the high desert region of eastern California, it would not be unreasonable to expect the use of both Yucca root and Devil's Claw in their pattern motifs. The author is also rather "shaky" on Kitanemuk twinned ware.

Kawaiisu

Coiling   Clockwise.

Willow, Yucca root, Bracken fern root, Devil's Claw (often hard to tell the difference), Bulrush (Tule) root, Sumac, Juncus (per Shirley Bauman of Tehachapi). Foundation of Deer Grass (may be large in diameter and mistaken for rods), never Red Bud or Sedge (per discussions with Dr. Moser).

Patterns: Often horizontal bands, isolated and connected Vees, "worms", stair steps, vertical "trees", or even a checkerboard. If a "bottle," it will have a small neck. The only American Indian tribe to use the "Grasshopper" (a.k.a "interrupted") stitch so common in Mesoamerica. This stitch is also found in some African countries (which proves conclusively that early man started in California, migrated to Mesoamerica, and later migrated to Africa where Mrs. Leakey dug up their bones)!!!

Twining   Willow warp and weft, Yucca or Tule root. Wefts may incorporate three, four, five, or even six warps, open or closed. Last several rows may be coiled. Twined water bottles are often painted with red ochre.

Foothill Yokuts

Coiling   Not common, probably clockwise.
Sedge, Willow, Red Bud, Bracken fern root, foundation of Deer Grass.

Patterns: Similar to Valley Yokuts or Western Monos; i.e., horizontally oriented motifs with simple geometrics; stair steps, zig zags, triangles, etc.

Twining   Sedge, Red Bud, Cottonwood (not common), Willow, Bracken fern root. Tules in receiving cradles. Patterns and techniques similar to Valley Yokuts or Western Mono. Shoulders often more arched on "jars." Snake pattern common. Extensive use of Sedge and Red Bud. Stair steps, zig zags, triangles, Red Bud and black Bracken fern root bands, may use chaparral for warps.

Sierra (Western) Mono

Coiling   Either direction.
Sedge, Bracken fern root, Red Bud, Chaparral, foundation of Deer Grass. Rim whip stitched or "self".

Patterns: Horizontal bands usually not bordered by a black or red coil, running (horizontally joined) Vees, rectangles, or hour glass (more common to Yokuts), zig zags, triangles often vertically oriented, may have pattern breaks (anomalies). Much black as compared with Foothill Yokuts, "deer hoof" motifs often small and in bands.

Twining   Same materials as coiling except Willow, Sumac, Chaparral, or Cottonwood for warps. Diagonal twining common, open twining on cradles. Occasional Soap Root coating particularly on cradles. Red Bud used extensively for pattern elements, particularly on cradles. Colored yarn frequently on cradle face protectors. Winnowers may have a wrapped rod of peeled Red Bud on rim. Patterns on twined ware are usually small and in bands.

Sierra Miwok

Coiling   Counterclockwise.

Sedge, Red Bud, Chaparral, Sumac, Creek Dogwood, Big Leaf Maple, Bracken fern root, Choke Cherry, possible Conifer root. One-rod or three-rod Willow foundation in north but Deer Grass foundation in the south. Rim often whip stitched, workmanship often only fair.

Patterns: Small, isolated running zig zags, up-down triangles, hour glass motifs.

Twining   Same materials as coiling but includes Willow, Chaparral, or Hazel warps. Wefts mostly Red Bud. Much open twining. Oval winnowers, usually minimal color, Red Bud or red Dogwood.

Plains or Coast Miwok

There seems to be several theories regarding the tribal name of those Indian folks who occupied the northern San Joaquin Valley in the Stockton-Sacramento valley floor. There is also a paucity of baskets from this region. Inasmuch as there is little reliable information or provenance on these baskets, there will be no discussion here.

Pomo

Coiling   Counterclockwise.

Sedge, Bulrush (Tule) root, Bracken fern root, Red Bud, Hazel, Big Leaf Maple, possible Dogwood, some Willow root, Pine root (various species), Woodwardia fern, feathers, beads, shells, one or three-rod Willow foundation, often boat-shaped.

Patterns: Pomo basket weavers were probably some of the most talented and varied of all California Indian weavers. They created many isolated or blocked triangles, stair steps, quail motif, many geometrics, zig zags, checkered, often feathered or beaded works. A "Dau" mark (a break in the pattern) is quite common.

Twined Various twining techniques, often very complex. Red Bud, Hazel, Dogwood, Pine root (*Pinus sabiniana, lambertiana, ponderosa,* or *jeffreyii*), Willow root, Woodwardia, Sedge root. Overlays rare. Their twining work is often quite complex even when using only plain two-strand twining.

Patwin

Coiling Counterclockwise.

Although there are believed to be many Patwin baskets extant, good provenance is usually limited. Because the Patwins are close neighbors of the Pomos and their basketry is quite similar, it is believed, by the author, that many Patwin baskets are mistakenly called Pomo. When authenticated, coiled Patwin baskets may have a one-rod Willow foundation and the stitching material may have a "knobby" appearance, possibly Horsetail fern root.

Twining Few twined Patwin baskets have been truly authenticated, ergo, little can be said at this point as to their characteristics.

Yuki

Coiling Clockwise.

Sedge (rare), Willow, Red Bud, Dogwood, Bear Grass, Big Leaf Maple, one-rod or three-rod Willow or Hazel foundation. A "Four Side" "start" is diagnostic. Workmanship is often substandard. They are the only northern California weavers who coil clockwise, and use the "Four Side" start, which is similar to a twining start.

Patterns: May have alternating red-white stitches or random dots or splotches (residual Red Bud bark), block or mottled geometrics, negative motifs, overlapping parallelograms, stair steps, or quail motifs. May be mistaken for Pomo or Nomlaki except usually with lesser quality and splotches.

Twined Uncommon. Mortar hoppers, seed beaters, or

burden baskets, usually crudely made. Dogwood, Conifer root, possible Grape rods.

Yurok

Coiling   Rare.

Twining   Willow, Hazel, Douglas Fir shoots (occasionally), Big Leaf Maple (occasionally), Bear Grass, Maidenhair fern, and Spruce root. Alder dyed Woodwardia stem, yellow dye from Wolf moss (rare). Horizontal rods of lattice twining for strength. Herringbone rim, half twist overlay (pattern only on the outside). Open or plain twining. Often lidded.

Patterns: Stair steps, butterflies, lightning, band of dashes, zig zags, similar to other "Klamath River people."

Hupa

Coiling   Not commonly used.

Twining   Similar to Yurok or Karok. There may be minor differences in top of hats but differences are hard to enumerate.

Karuk

Coiling   Not commonly used.

Twining   Hazel, Sand Bar Willow shoots and roots, Maidenhair fern, Alder dyed Woodwardia stems, quills, Bear Grass, Pine root, Grape root.

Patterns: Stair step designs, lids often with knob. Similar to other "Klamath River" tribes except much Willow root and Grape root.

Wintu

Coiling   Not commonly used.

Twining   Willow, Sedge root, Hazel, Conifer shoots and roots (probably *Pinus sabiniana*), Bear Grass, Maidenhair fern, Tule, Woodwardia fern, quills, Willow root, Red Bud. Full twist overlay (yields pattern on both sides).

Patterns: Bands common in Woodwardia fern, spirals downright, quail motifs, stair steps with "flint" points, spiraling rectangles. Workmanship often only fair. May resemble Maidu work.

Modoc
Coiling   Not commonly used.

Twining   Tule (Bulrush) fibers and weaver strands for warp and weft, Conifer root, Cattail leaves often twisted to form cordage used in twining or household uses. Conifer root used similar to twisted Cattail leaves. Rim may be bent over or scalloped. Nettle fiber rarely used as "start" and first several inches on hats.

Patterns: Dyed Tule fibers. Full twist overlay. Baskets and cradles are usually pliable due to flexibility of twisted cordage.

Achumawi ("Pit River")
Coiling   Not commonly used.

Twining   Hazel or Willow warps, Pine root wefts, Bear Grass, Maidenhair fern, Chaparral, Red Bud, Tule, Bulrush root, and Bracken fern root. Big Leaf Maple may be present (hard to recognize). Base may have lattice weave for strength, and may be concave.

Patterns: Many triangles, Vees, and diamonds. Stair step downright, Vees upright. Checkered motif. Base cross warped, may have dark Willow rod at rim. Full twist overlay. Workmanship not always good. May resemble Modocs, but better!

Atsugewi ("Hat Creek")
Coiling   Not commonly used.

Twining   Chaparral, Pine root, Bear Grass, Maidenhair fern, Possible Red Bud, Willow or Hazel warps, Big Leaf Maple. Full Twist overlay. Cross warps near base, then three-strand twining, may have lattice weave on inside at base, possible Willow rod or flush at rim.

Patterns: "Butterflies", stair steps with quail plumes, or Flints. Similar to Pit River except usually better workmanship. Similar to Maidu except not as good.

Yana
Coiling   Rare.

Twining   Baskets are rare but when located materials are believed to include Big Leaf Maple, Pine root, Red Bud, Bear Grass, Willow or Hazel warps with Sedge root or Pine root wefts. Tule (Cattail rare) on receiving cradles.

Patterns: Either in Red Bud or a black unspecified plant (possibly mud dyed Red Bud), rarely isolated. Vertical chevrons with quail plume or flints, horizontal mountains and valleys, stacked triangles slightly resembling the Maidu motifs.

Maidu (*)

Coiling   Counterclockwise.

Sedge root, three-rod Willow, Red Bud, Big Leaf Maple, Bracken fern root, Maidenhair fern, "Lump Root" (poss. Briar root), Pine root (*P. sabiniana, lambertiana, ponderosa,* or *jeffreyii*), Bear Grass, black may be dyed Red Bud, Creek Dogwood, possible Tule root. Full twist overlay. Stitches usually short and bifurcated on non-work side (diagnostic of Maidu baskets). Tule used for domestic items.

Patterns: Many triangles (up, down, spiraling), diamonds, stair steps with flints, "snakes head", butterflies, quail plume motif, extensive Red Bud pattern. Usually good workmanship.

Twining   Conifer root, Bracken fern root, occasionally Douglas Fir shoots, Five Fingered (Maidenhair) fern, Buck Brush, Willow, Red Bud, and Hazel. Patterns consist mostly of triangles and diamonds in band, zig zags, or lightning.

(*) Maidu, as discussed herein, includes the Konkow, Northern (Mountain) Maidu, and the Nisenan.

Washoe

Coiling   Counterclockwise.

Willow, Willow foundation, Red Bud, Bracken fern root, Sunburned Willow (rare), Dogwood, Bulrush root, Big Leaf Maple, one-rod and three-rod Willow (foundation), spent running end occasionally tucked under like "Mission" stitch.

Whip stitch at rim. Fag ends clipped.

Patterns: Many fancy basket motifs, often isolated but small and vertically oriented. Stair step, many triangles, motifs often tall and slender. Frequently glass beads over one-rod Willow.

Twining   Willow warps and wefts, Sunburned Willow (rare), Red Bud, Bracken Fern root or Bulrush root.

Patterns: Often rather austere, as contrasted to coiled basketry. In twining, weaver often wove left-to-right, then flipped basket over, or up-side-down, and again left-to-right. This yields a snake-like orientation of the weft with sap and heart wood side of weft alternating on outside.

Paiute (*)

Coiling   Counterclockwise.

Willow on Willow foundation, Bracken fern root, Red Bud, Sunburned Willow, Devil's Claw, Sedge root, Bulrush root. Possibly Creek Dogwood. Rim often whip stitched. Mouth of jars may be proportionally small.

Patterns: Mono Lake Paiute may resemble Washo fancy baskets while Owens Valley Paiutes are more austere. Washoe do not normally use Bulrush root. Many use Sunburned Willow.

Twining   Twining was apparently quite common, albeit the amount of extant twined ware is minimal except for plain twined water bottles, which are usually torpedo shaped and coated with pine pitch.

(*) Includes Northern, Pyramid Lake, Mono Lake, and Owens Valley Paiutes. Each have minor differences in patterns and style but their materials are similar.

Panamint

Coiling   Clockwise.

Willow, Devil's Claw, Red Bud (only last fifty +/- years), rarely Sedge, Yucca root, Bracken fern root, Juncus (*J. cooperii* or *balticus*), Bulrush root (natural or dyed black), Quills, three-rod Willow or two-rod plus a bundle (foundation).

Grass foundation in older baskets, rim ticking or whipped stitch at terminal. Shapes may include Yokuts-style jars, "mortuary" style jars, deep basin storage baskets similar to the Yokuts or the Western Monos.

Patterns: Some resemble Valley Yokuts, some resemble Chemehuevi. Zoomorphs, birds, or Big Horn sheep quite common, bird quills common. May include anthropomorphs. Body patterns often enclosed by black bands. May have black band near rim and vertical black stripe(s) bordering wide vertical or slanting geometric motifs. Those made by the Hansen family may have extensive Juncus with mostly vertically oriented triangles or tall skinny diamonds either isolated or enclosed in black bands (per Eva Slater).

Twining   Willow warp and weft, similar to Owens Valley Paiutes. Although many twined baskets were made, not many are extant.

Tribes of the Southwestern USA

The primary thrust of this bundle of words was originally to address Indian basketry plants of California and the western Great Basin. However, after reflecting upon some of the plants used by southern and central California weavers, it became obvious that some of those plants were also used by tribes in Arizona. Ditto, plants used by Arizona Indians are similar to those used by native basketmakers in New Mexico.

Inasmuch as this author did not want to slight the Southwest people, the scope was expanded to include Arizona and New Mexico, which are referred to herein categorically as the Southwest people. Because pottery and cloth weaving seems to have been more favored by the earlier Southwest Indian people, basketry did not play the dominant role it did in California or the Pacific Northwest. Therefore, the number of Southwest tribes considered herein was minimized. It must be emphasized that because the number of tribes is minimized in this treatise, there is absolutely no inference that basketry in the Southwest was subordinate to that of other areas in western North America.

Inasmuch as the author's knowledge of Southwestern pottery and fabric weaving is only slightly greater than his knowledge of brain surgery, he concentrated his efforts on Southwestern basketry. His first hand knowledge of Southwest basketry, and their plant materials, is based upon his personal collection of both baskets and cradles from this region, augmented and tweaked by conversations with basket makers, basket collectors, botanists, "experts" and some "not-so-experts."

Although the area occupied by the Southwestern people is huge, the number of tribes is relatively small, as compared with California, and those that practiced extensive basketry is even smaller. However, their basketry is often very fine quality, as discussed on the following pages.

Tohono O'odham (Formerly called Papago)

Coiling Counterclockwise.

Yucca leaf (*Y. elata*) stitching, and Devil's Claw for black. Willow or Cottonwood (older pieces), Cattail (rarely), Bear Grass (*Nolina*) foundation. White, yellow and green Yucca leaves make up the large flattened whorls. Devil's Claw for black with Yucca root (*Y. bacata*) for the red pattern motifs. Prior to circa 1920, Willow as a stitching material. However, Willow is not as common on the reservation as it is elsewhere in Arizona. Consequently, post 1920 baskets rarely contain Willow as a stitching material.

Patterns: Motifs run the gamut from simple geometrics to complex anthropomorphs or zoomorphs. "Figure Four" starts are reportedly after about 1920. Within the last several decades, use of horse hair has become popular in creating very spectacular and intricate patterns, including "Elder Brother," lizards, rattlesnakes, cactus, etc. The "split stitch" is often used to create a pattern.

Twining   Not commonly used except for water bottles.

Note: In the last half of the 20th century, there were rumored to be nearly 2,000 Tohono O'odham basket makers creating baskets, more than all of the rest of the USA, combined.

Akimel O'otham   (Formerly known as Pima)

Note spelling is O'otham as contrasted with O'odham for Papagos.

Coiling   Counterclockwise.

Willow stitching, Devil's Claw, may have Cattail bundle, possible Cottonwood stitching, Willow three-rod or Bear Grass foundation (mostly rods foundation). If stitching is Yucca leaf, the basket may be Tohono O'odham.

Patterns: Almost always solid black center (almost diagnostic of Akimel baskets), Frets common. Isolated vertical motifs, zig zags, running mountains, stair step rectangles. Rims may be black. Much more Willow than Tohono O'odham.

Walapai (Hualapai)

Coiling   Rare.

Three-rod Sumac, Devil's Claw, Yucca root, or Mountain Mahogany root.

Patterns: Generally simple or plain geometric forms such as zig zags, stripes, bands or chevrons, either vertical, diagonal, or horizontal.

Twining   Sumac weft and warp, often slant warp, mostly diagonal twining with Sumac bark on warps and as a pattern. Wefts occasionally unpeeled Sumac, black is mostly dyed Sumac. Some Yucca root, Devil's Claw (not common), Mt. Mahogany. Wrapped two-rod rim, squat, flat, or even deeply concaved bottomed bowls which belly out rather low.

Patterns: Most generally a horizontal band of checkered dyed black and peeled Sumac. Workmanship is generally only fair and ware is mostly utilitarian, but very strong and durable.

Havasupai

Coiling   Counterclockwise coiling is believed to be no earlier than circa 1890. Willow on three-rod Willow, Devil's Claw, and occasionally Sumac. Unlike Akimel O'otham, the "start" is not black Devil's Claw. Base is often concave.

Patterns: Similar to Western Apache except more "dainty" (per Turnbaugh). Anthropomorphs, zoomorphs. May have black or herringbone rim, radiating zig zags, stacked triangles or rectangles. May have seven point star in center.

Twining   Plain or diagonal twining of Willow or Cottonwood, Devil's Claw, or Sumac.

Patterns: May be bold black but less complex than Western Apache, concentric circles, radial lines of single geometric motifs, zig zags, "cogged line" (running mountains), some anthropomorphs or zoomorphs.

Yavapai

Coiling   Counterclockwise.

Yavapai people lived at one time on the same Rez (reservation) as the Western Apache, and thus they influenced, and were influenced by, each other. The two tribes make very similar coiled baskets, except the Yavapai may use more bold and solid black, or small checkered rectangles ("mountain crystals") or triangles. Rims are usually alternating black/tan and their patterns similar but more bold and "heavy" but less complex than Western Apaches. Willow on three-rod Willow, Devil's Claw, Sumac occasionally, some *Yucca elata* leaves.

Patterns: Very similar to Western Apache except there may be more fine checkered tan and black. Anthropomorphs/zoomorphs common, dogs not uncommon.

Twining   Very similar to Western Apache. This twining

is generally more coarse than in Northern California.

Western Apache (White Mountain, San Carlos, Tonto).

Coiling   Counterclockwise.

Willow on three-rod Willow, Devil's Claw, Sumac, some Yucca (*Y. elata*)

Patterns: Large Xs, zoomorphs, anthropomorphs, stars, triangles, diamonds, horizontal rows/ blocks of connected Vees, stacked rectangles, black centers similar to the Akimel O'otham, many ollas, large and small, very complex and "busy" pattern motifs. Dogs, horses and people are often used profusely.

Twining   Plain, diagonal, and three-strand. Vertical warps of Willow or Sumac. Flat bottomed or torpedo shaped jars with wood lugs and pine pitch waterproofing.

Patterns: Horizontal bands of checkered Sumac bark or Devil's Claw, much buckskin and metal cones on burden baskets. Design motifs on twining similar to, but less complex or busy than, coiled ware.

Mescalero Apache

Coiled   Counterclockwise.

Willow on three-rod Willow, possibly two rods plus a bundle. Yucca leaf with or without aniline dye. Devil's Claw occasionally.

Patterns: Large five or six pointed concentric stars on circular trays are common. Dogs (possibly horses) in black on Yucca leaf. Motifs are usually small and isolated, often in aniline dye, some rim ticking. Coils are normally large resulting in a corduroy surface.

Twining   Not common.

Jicarilla Apache

Coiling   Counterclockwise.

Yucca leaf, Sumac, or Willow over Willow rods foundation, aniline dye, often faded. Coils are thick and not flattened, as in Tohono O'odham basketry. Rim may have whip stitch or false braiding. Stitching is generally quite coarse. Similar to Mescalero Apache.

Patterns: Five pointed stars in black dye very common. Zoomorphs or anthropomorphs uncommon.

Twining   Not common.

Hopi, Second Mesa
Coiling   Counterclockwise.

Sometimes known as "Middle Mesa", as contrasted with First or Third Mesa Hopi. Yucca leaf (*Y. angustifolia*) over a Galetta grass (*Hilaria jamesii*) foundation. Coils are quite large in diameter with long slender stitches. Terminals are usually abrupt and "starts" are of the "bent finger" style.

Patterns: Stitching material is gaily dyed generally with vegetal but sometimes aniline dyes. Colors are vivid when fresh but often fade with exposure to sun or light. Motifs mainly depict katsinas (kachinas), ears of corn or cactus.

Twining   Not common.

Hopi, Third Mesa
Coiling   Not common.

Twining   Not common.

Wicker   Hopis are some of the few Western US Indians who use wicker as a primary weaving style. Wicker may extend to all of the Hopi villages but the Third Mesa weavers use it almost exclusively. Warps are of Dune-broom (*Parryella filigolia*), Sumac, Willow, or Rabbit Bush (*Chrysothamus spp.*). Wefts are usually of Yucca. Many weavers create plaques, open work, "sifting trays", or "piki" trays.

Patterns: Those on wicker ware are normally gaily colored (dyed) katsinas, or occasionally corn or desert plants; e.g., yuccas or cacti.

Navajo

Coiling	Counterclockwise.

Sumac over three-rod Sumac

Most Navajo baskets seen on the market or in collections today are the so-called *Navajo Wedding* Tray, sometimes referred to as a *Sing basket*, most of which were made, not by Navajos but by the Southern Utes. Those made by Navajos are also of Sumac over a three- rod Sumac foundation.

Patterns: Most Wedding Trays consist of a multi-pointed star in the center with a "spirit line" leading from the center to the edge. Those baskets made by Navajo weavers may also be Wedding Trays but are more often shallow to deep basins with perhaps three or four large *coyote tracks* (similar to the Chevrolet auto logo). Color of the motif may be red dye or even red ochre.

Twined   Not commonly used. Some water ollas may be twined of peeled or even whole Sumac, and coated with pine pitch.

Tribes of the Pacific Northwest, Canada and Alaska

In the previous section it was stated that the original thrust of this treatise was to address Indian basketry of California and maybe the western edge of the Great Basin; i.e., those Indian tribes contiguous to or partly within California. After reflecting on materials used by Arizona Indians, as compared with southern California Indian weavers, the regional scope was extended into Arizona and a bit into New Mexico. Well... the same murky logic applies to northern California and Oregon; i.e., many of the Oregon Indian basketmakers use the same materials as do those in northwestern California. Therefore, for the same reason as previously stated, the decision was made to expand the region of discussion into Oregon.

But... tribal practices along the Oregon side of the Columbia River are not much different from those on the

Washington side, Right? Therefore, the scope was tweaked a wee bit more to include eastern Washington and the "Plateau." Anyone familiar with the Pacific Northwest recognizes that basketry in northwestern Oregon isn't that much different from southwestern Washington so the scope was expanded north into the Olympic Peninsula.

Next, a look at basketry materials in the Puget Sound region shows that basketry of the Makah people of Washington (USA) is almost the same as the Nootka of British Columbia (Canada). Therefore, the Nootka were included as well. Some basket collectors say the Makah and Nootka are so closely related they are almost one tribe. Also, the inland Salish baskets of eastern Washington (USA) are similar to the inland Salish of British Columbia (Canada), so they were included as well.

Regarding some Haida and Tlingit weavers, these people are part of the United States (Alaska), and you can't ignore them just because it snows a lot and their ground is frozen much of the time. The same can be said about the Aleuts and Eskimos, so they are included also. If one is to jump from Washington to Alaska, there is a whole lot of area in between, like in British Columbia (Canada), so those tribes were also included.

Considering southern Alaska and British Columbia wouldn't be fair if northern Alaska were excluded, so Eskimos were also included. Fortunately, the North Pole got in the way and the northern expansion either had to stop or 1) extend into the aura borealis, or 2) fall over the edge, or 3) fall down the other side. However, Eskimo people extend all the way across the northern edge of Canada, so a few of these people were also included just so that the Canadian government wouldn't get insulted.

Much of the information regarding Pacific Northwest Indian basketry has been gleaned from the literature, backed up by inspection of scores of actual baskets, either from the author's personal collection, which represents almost every tribe discussed herein, or from visits to museums or private collections all over this Land of Eternal Sunshine. Some students of the Pacific Northwest and Alaska may take umbrage at the inclusion, or lack thereof, of specific tribes, but because the regions is so vast, and the number of individual tribes is so large, specific tribes were selected based upon the popularity of their baskets in known collections, rather than romanticism often associated with specific tribes. Also, tribal names change almost as fast as does the stock market, so tribal names mention herein may not be technically correct on the day the reader picks up this document. Names selected for inclusion herein are based primarily upon how they are referred to by basket collectors, not by ethnologists or stock brokers.

Southern Oregon

Coiling   Not commonly used.

Twining   Those baskets created along the Pacific coast of southern Oregon are frequently very similar, plant material-wise, to baskets created by the Tolowa of northern California; i.e., Spruce root and Hazel warps/wefts are used extensively, either in close twining/cross-warp or open twining for utility baskets. When decorated, they are similar to northern California baskets in their use of Maidenhair fern, Woodwardia fern, and Bear Grass.

Patterns: Patterns are similar to those from northern California.

Nez Perce

Coiling   Not commonly used.

Twining   Most twined ware consists either of "fez" type hats of Willow, Cottonwood, Cotton twine, Cherry bark, or commercial yarn. The "start" of some hats utilizes the "hide tie" style where a buckskin cord is used to tie the warps together and then hangs down the sides as an ornamental "drop." Flat or "soft" bags (often referred to as "Sally Bags") are quite common and utilize corn husks, cotton twine, and Indian Hemp.

Patterns: Motifs on hats are often deep Vees, while those on flat bags are almost always isolated geometrics, but busy. Motifs on the front are almost always different from on those on the back. Colors are often quite vivid when fresh, but tend to fade with time.

Yakima

Coiling   Clockwise.

Baskets are normally cylindrical in shape and composed of Cedar bark for both foundation and stitching, although some coiled ware has Cattail foundations. Rims are often "looped" or "scalloped" similar to the Klickitat or Inland Salish. Pattern material is Cherry bark, or Bear Grass, often dyed.

Patterns: Like many Plateau tribes, basketry is commonly imbricated. In this regard, Yakima baskets resemble many of the Plateau or Inland Salish weavings.

Twining   The Yakima, like many Plateau weavers, created flat Sally Bags, similar to the Nez Perce or Wishram people.

Wishram/Wasco

Coiling   Not common, although some are imbricated coiled baskets, similar to other Plateau baskets.

Twining   Like the Yakima baskets, many twined Wasco or Wishram baskets are cylindrical in shape and actually more a bag than a rigid basket. Plain and dyed Tules or rushes are often used as wefts together with cotton string or Indian Hemp.

Patterns: Flat bags are similar to the Nez Perce or Yakima except that patterns are usually quite intricate with many triangles, slashes, zig zags, zoomorphs and anthropomorphs with horizontal diamond faces, big eyes, and "X ray" ribs/bones. In some cases the face occupies almost the entire face of the bag. Twined hats are very similar to those of the Nez Perce; i.e., the "fez" type with a leather ("hide") tie and side dangle.

Klickitat

Coiling   Clockwise.

Conifer (Spruce and Cedar) root foundation

and stitching, imbrication of Cherry bark and Bear Grass. Occasionally Equisetum (Horsetail) fern root dyed black. Horsetail fern root is often "lumpy" and resembles a knobby black Bracken fern root. Rims are noticeably scalloped and sides flare outward, taller than diameter of the mouth. Stitches are interlocking. Bottoms often rectangular, the sides becoming rounded as they progress up the sides.

Patterns: Deep Vees or butterflies with "flint", similar to "quail plumes", or rectangular motifs. Some zoomorphs and anthropomorphs, zig zags, diagonal or vertical bold motifs such as *salmon gills, geese-in-flight*, etc.

Note: Okanogan and Wenatchee weavers made similar imbricated baskets. Theirs are also taller than the diameter of the mouth but their bases are usually oval with a flat face/backs and sides that curve outward, then straight upward.

Chehalis

Coiling   Clockwise.

These are the westernmost people in the Columbia River region who use imbricated coiling. They used the outer edge of a Cattail leaf for part of the imbrication element, also Bear Grass and wild Cherry bark.

Patterns: Not unlike the Klickitat except not quite so busy.

Twining   Spruce root warp and weft, half-twist overlay of Bear Grass and Cattail. Aniline dye common.

Patterns: X-ray anthropomorphs similar to the Wishram or Wasco. Although some authorities claim Cattail was used as a pattern material, the author has cause to question the use of Cattails for such use.

Quinault/Quileute

Coiling   Not common.

Twining   These baskets along the ocean, or west side of

the Olympic Peninsula are quite similar to those produced by the Makah and Nootka; i.e., plain or wrapped twining with overlays of Maidenhair fern, Bracken fern root, Bear Grass, plaited Cedar bark bottom, and Cedar bark warps. Occasionally weavers used Willow bark, and wild Cherry bark. Most baskets made for sale are short, often with a lid. Larger baskets may have scallop or braided rim. Most twining is rather finely done.

Patterns: Unlike the Makah and Nootka baskets, which have nautical patterns, these baskets usually have horizontal bands or zig zags of brightly dyed geometric motifs, but normally no nautical motifs. Large baskets may have an anthropomorphic or zoomorphic band just under the rim. The Cedar root bottom splints are usually quite wide and almost always fully plaited. These splints are then split into three or more segments which become vertical warps.

Makah, Nootka

Coiling   Not common.

Twining   Bases are plaited, with wide Cedar root splints which are split, then become vertical continuation (warps) of the basal splints. Wefts of Cedar bark, Bear Grass, Woodwardia fern, Maidenhair fern, Bracken fern root. Wrapped twining.

Patterns: Often dyed Bear Grass rather than overlay, cross warp. Occasionally wide Cedar splint just under the rim. Nautical scenes of boats, whaling, fish etc. are the norm. Colors are of aniline dye which fades easily. Hats are usually "onion top," pitched, oriental looking; i.e., sloping, with nautical scenes.

Fraser River, Thompson River, Lillooet

Coiling   Clockwise.

These baskets are often referred to collectively as *Inland Salish* or lumped as *Thompson River.* All three tribes use partial or fully imbricated coiled basketry with wide, flat Cedar bark splint foundations (Western Red Cedar most often) similar to the Makah or Nootka. Stitching is wide Cedar Bark over which is imbricated Cherry bark, Bear Grass, Spruce root (*Picea engelmanii*), or Woodwardia fern.

Patterns: Mostly broad geometric motifs in imbrication. Often the entire surface is imbricated. Coils are usually quite broad, almost 1/2 inch wide, and almost always quite flat. Cherry bark seems to be a favorite pattern material. In "coffin-like" cradles, patterns on one side are different from those on the opposite side.

Twining   Not common.

Tsimshian, Kwakiutl

Coiling   Not common.

Twining   Cedar and Spruce root warps and wefts, Bear Grass, and Maidenhair fern. Normal twining is not as common as is plaiting or In-Between twining. Although twining is the more common weaving style throughout the Pacific Northwest, plaiting is not uncommon, particularly on the flat bases. Cedar root splints are used for both the bottoms and sides, or even the tops, including a plaited top knob. In-Between twining is a process in which one coil is plaited with no twisted weft, and the next coil is plain twining using two weft strands, usually in Cedar or Spruce root, which results in a rather checkered pattern with the vertical members flat and wide, and horizontal member twisted and narrow.

Patterns: Pattern elements are often rather subdued, linear in mud-dyed black Cedar bark or aniline dyed Bear Grass in false embroidery. In the latter case, there is usually minimal Bear Grass with either plain plaiting or In-Between twining. Bear Grass and Maidenhair fern are used, similar to the Tlingits.

Haida / Tlingit

Coiling   Not commonly used.

Twining   Spruce root warp and weft, "Grass" (*Glyceria striate spp.*), Maidenhair fern, Bear Grass, Woodwardia fern. Most work is plain twining, albeit three strand twining is often used to add strength and rigidity. Haida often place a row of three strand twining near the base and bend over and bind under warps at the rim, whereas Tlingit often leave the warps exposed at the terminal.

Patterns: Although the two tribes are similar in materials and weaving styles, their patterns are often quite different. Haida baskets often show "skip-stitch", which forms a pattern in contrast. They also may have one or several horizontal bands of "skip-stitch" near the rim, whereas Tlingit baskets are usually well patterned with much Maidenhair fern and plain or dyed Bear Grass motifs of false embroidery. Both are usually moderate to small and almost always cylindrical in shape. Haida baskets are often woven with the basket vertical and "up-side-down." Both Cedar and Spruce roots are utilized, the Spruce being lighter and shinier than Cedar root.

Plaiting   Both tribes make extensive use of plaiting. Western Red Cedar seems to be favored. These baskets may somewhat resemble those by the Tsimshian or Kwakiutl.

Aleut

Coiling   Not commonly used.

Twining   Beach (Rye) Grass, commercial yarn, possibly Bear Grass, seal gut, seal skin, feathers, open or closed plain and three strand twining, and false embroidery. Rim may be braided with square loops. Open and cross warps. Rarely rattle tops. Frequently has a row of three-strand twining near the base and at the "turn."

Patterns: The Attu and Aleuts probably make the finest and most delicate basketry in the USA, or perhaps the world. Their stitch count is almost unbelievable, it often being finer and more delicate than most fine silk cloth. These weavers are famous for their "wallets" of fold-over weavings, incorporating wool or commercial yarn, some of which have aniline dye and fade badly. Motifs are usually similar to commercial cloth; i.e., in bands or isolated but usually all-encompassing.

Western Eskimo

Coiling   Clockwise.

Because these baskets tend toward simplicity in their design and patterns, they were rarely collected and displayed, and thus are usually rather scarce in museums and private holdings. When located, they are often mistaken for baskets either from the Orient or from Mesoamerica. They are usually well worn and recognizable as Eskimo only by the seal gut pattern elements. The primary stitching material, "Beach (rye) Grass," resembles some Mesoamerican materials or raffia, which is an exotic (imported) fiber. Silk or wool yarn, dyed seal skin or gut are diagnostic, as are large bundle foundations. Baskets are frequently globular or nearly round, most often with a lid which usually has a round or tear-drop shaped knob. Because Beach Grass does not wear well, it may resemble well worn raffia. If lidded, the shape tends toward being tall with a low hip and somewhat pointed top.

Patterns: Frequently small and isolated x's or small geometric motifs in worsted yarn or rarely in seal gut, or some commercial material. If the dye is aniline, it is very frequently faded and may be visible only on the inside where it is protected from sunlight.

Twining   Twining was not the forte of most Western Eskimos, although some utility baskets incorporated twining in their construction. When a twined basket is located, in all likelihood it is rather coarsely made and has minimal pattern motifs.

Labrador Eskimo (northeastern Canada)

Coiling   Clockwise.

Although this treatise was supposed to end at the North Pole, the author just couldn't resist the temptation to include the Labrador Eskimo, primarily because these baskets are so often overlooked as a North American basketry form. If the truth be known, there are a heap of baskets out there that are considered Oriental or Mesoamerican that are actually Eskimo, from that part of Canada north of Hudson's Bay, not in Greenland, and south of the polar ice cap. The author has several very fine examples in his collection. Without exception they are "gap-stitched" gift bowls, often lidded, with the grass foundation shamelessly exposed. The foundation material is unknown to the author, as is also the stitching material. A casual glance at the weaver strand would suggest that the weaver used a form of "Bound Under Fag End Stitch" (BUFES). Frequently, the basket is lidded but sans a knob. There may also be a coiled handle that is usually broken or detached.

CHAPTER 4

SPECIFIC BASKETRY PLANTS

Over the many years (or is it decades) that the author has been collecting, creating, learning, and teaching about western US Indian basketry, it has become quite evident that many Indian basketry devotees know pitifully little about the materials used to create baskets, or cradles. Some collectors, and even some dealers or museum staff members, merely "waltz around" the subject and take for granted some other person's idea as to the name of the originating tribe, the plants used, and even the name of the basket creator. When quizzed about the basketry materials, the subject often gets changed very rapidly, or a puzzled look suddenly appears. This is because not a whole lot of people are intimately familiar with what a specific plant material looks like after it finds its way into a basket, particularly if the plant material was harvested 100 years ago.

Therefore, the narrative that follows, addresses a few of the more commonly used plant species used by western North American Indians in their basket making; thirty-seven species to be exact. Because the subject was arbitrarily limited to western North America, discussion of plants used by other tribes will be kind of hinted at only. The plants considered herein are listed in the Table of Contents, and again in chapter two. They are addressed in alphabetical order of the common, not botanical name; e.g., Alder is used rather than *Alnus*. In each case, photographs are presented of the plants, as they may be found growing in the field, and again as they appear in a basket, or cradle. A narrative is also included to discuss how the plant was gathered, cured, processed, and utilized.

Gathering native plants can be a bit tricky if you aren't

sure of the plant you are gathering. Your author has thirty (plus a bunch more) years experience under his overly ample belt. Two years ago he gathered a nice batch of Sumac and was splitting it, trying to impress a friend, when he discovered it was not Sumac after all, but beautiful shoots of poison oak. Don't you do a dumb thing like that! Not to worry however, he's an Indian and you know what they say about Indians and poison oak! (It's true... sometimes). A gathering hazard.... Whenever you want to gather materials, like Sumac, remember, you will be entering rattlesnake country and you had better let Mr. or Mrs. R. Snake know your intentions before you set foot in the brush. Remember, it is the home of Mr. or Mrs. R. Snake and they may not welcome your intrusion.

The following is a plant-by-plant discussion of some of the basketry materials used by western North American Indians. Most of the botanical information on plants was gleaned from Jepson, Moerman, Moser, Cain, practicing basket weavers, hearsay, gossip, hunches, speculation, guesses, and, on some occasions actual knowledge. Although there are many more plants that could have been included, the plant materials selected for discussion herein cover the lion's share of plants used in basket making all over the West, the Southwest and the Northwest.

Alder Bark *(Alnus spp.)*

Alder, as a shoot, a root, or as a weaver strand, is not commonly used to create a basket or cradle. However, its bark is used extensively as a reddish brown dye for Woodwardia stems (Giant Chain fern) throughout the Pacific Northwest, from about San Francisco, north into coastal Canada. Woodwardia fern stems, as a weaving material, are addressed later in more detail. These current paragraphs are devoted to Alder bark and its use in connection with Woodwardia ferns.

In most regions of North America, there are plant materials that have either black, red, yellow, or various colored bark or roots, and are (were) used to create basketry patterns; e.g., Red Bud, basal red Juncus, Bracken fern root, Devil's Claw, etc. Where such native plant materials were not available, vegetal, or even commercial dyes were often used to create a pattern material. Alder bark is one of the more commonly used vegetal dyes.

Alder bark is obtained by stripping off bark from the tree trunk and allowing it to age and darken to a reddish brown, or by boiling a portion of pounded bark to extract the dye. It has been rumored about that some early 20th century weavers chewed the bark, which also coated it with saliva, and then ran the Woodwardia weaver strand through their mouth to create the reddish brown color. The saliva is reported to serve as a mordant which sets the dye and makes it colorfast. Using the mouth to dye weaver strands may have been effective but it sure was dissuasive of husbands and/or lovers! Some current basket weavers, such as Verna Reece, of Happy Camp, Siskiyou County, California, contend this is just an old wive's tale so please don't pass it on as

gospel. However, the tale was told to the author a number of times by a number of "experts" and occurs occasionally in the literature.

For those not familiar with Alder trees outside of a tree zoo, Figure 1 depicts several Alder trees in the wilds of Siskiyou County with Verna Reece of Happy Camp and Bruce Hobaugh of North Bend Oregon, in the lower front for perspective.

Alder bark tends to turn reddish brown within a few minutes

*Figure 1. Alder trees near Happy Camp.
Siskiyou County, California.*

Figure 2. Verna Reece and Bruce Hobaugh
harvesting alder bark. Note the rusty red on the tree trunk
between the two. The bark's cut was opened only
several minutes before the picture was taken.

after being harvested, but is often boiled (or ? chewed) for a few minutes before using the solution as a dye. Verna Reece claims (personal conversation) the best dye comes from bark on the north side of a tree.

Although many plant materials will take a dye, weaver strands from Woodwardia ferns are far and away the more popular subjects. Details of Woodwardia fern wefts are addressed later in this treatise.

Bear Grass *(Nolina microcarpa)* Arizona and New Mexico

Please note that there are two basketry plants addressed herein as Bear Grass. One is a *Nolina*, related to the Agaves or Yuccas, and is used extensively in Arizona and New Mexico as a foundation material. The other is a low growing lily-like plant used for false embroidery throughout the Pacific Northwest. The Bear Grass considered at this point is *Nolina microcarpa*, as used in Arizona and New Mexico. The second Bear Grass, *Xerophyllum tenax*, is treated later.

First, a few words regarding the botanical name *microcarpa*. Anyone who speaks at least a spattering of the King's English knows that the word *micro* generally denotes something small, as contrasted with *macro*, meaning large. The term carpa is often used by botany-type folks in reference to a plant's leaf or fruit. Ergo, *microcarpa* would suggest the leaf or fruit is small. In the case of Bear Grass, the "small" might suggest that the width (not the length) of the leaf is small, as contrasted to the related Yuccas or Agaves. A Bear Grass leaf wider than about 3/8 inch and 1/8 inch thick is rare, as contrasted to some Yucca leaves which may be an inch or so wide at the base, and 1/2 to 3/4 inch thick. An Agave leaf is often several inches wide and an inch or more thick. The smallness of microcarpa, however, does not apply to the leaf's length, which may be in excess of four feet long.

Virtually every coiled Tohono O'odham (formerly called Papago) basket created within the last half century contains a foundation of Bear Grass, which is really not a grass at all. When viewed in the wild, Bear Grass looks very similar to a Yucca and is part of the *Nolina*, or Agave family as are many of the Yuccas. They differ from most Yuccas in that they do not stand upright and their leaves are much thinner and long, slender, drooping leaves, giving the impression that a Mexican fighting bull recently visited the plant to practice man-fighting, as suggested in Fig 3. Most Yuccas or Agaves have stout, stiff elongated leaves that are usually arranged in a whorl about the stalk. Arizona Bear Grass, however, has long, slender, drooping leaves, giving the impression that a Mexican fighting bull recently visited the plant to practice man-fighting, as suggested in Fig 3.

Figure 3. Arizona Bear Grass at Tuzigoot Park Headquarters near Sedona, Arizona.

The Tohono O'odham and a few of the other Southwest Indian weavers split the long slender leaves into thin strips and included them into a relatively fat bundle foundation. In most baskets, the foundation was wrapped by strands of split Yucca leaves (*Yucca elata*). Some Tohono O'odham weavers used a split stitch which resembles a wide open Vee, as shown in Figure 5. Tuzigoot Park headquarters is just southwest of Sedona, in north central Arizona.

Under a magnifier, Bear Grass looks like it is composed of many longitudinal fibers cemented by a green pulp. The green is often retained and visible in the foundation of a coiled basket. Figure 4 depicts an open field in Prescott Valley in north central Arizona. The larger tree in the left-central portion of the photo is a Juniper (locally called a Cedar), while the smaller clumps on the right and in front of the Juniper are Bear Grass. Note that the man fighting bull apparently visited them also.

Figure 4. Bear Grass in a Prescott Valley, Arizona, field. The larger tree is a Juniper and the Bear Grass is in front of the tree, and again in the foreground.

Figure 5 is a detail of a Bear Grass foundation in a Tohono O'odham basket. This photo was taken with a macro lens at 2x, which was then enlarged to its present size. The enlargement is intended to show details of the material after it finds its way into the foundation of a basket. Bear Grass is the horizontal material, and could be described as being rather pulpy/fibrous.

Bear Grass is a dark forest green, until the leaves are amputated from the plant. That green is then bleached by placing it the direct desert sun. However, if it is split longitudinally into slivers, the core's outer green surface may be covered up by the pulpy inner material, which is a light sandy color.

Figure 5. A detail photo of Bear Grass as it occurs in the foundation of a Tohono O'odham basket, and covered by Yucca elata stitching material using a "Split Stitch."

In most cases, Tohono baskets have very thick coils, which are reportedly pounded while still wet. In the subject basket, which is a gift from Bob Hickman of The Gallery of the Old West, in Old Sacramento, the foundation is almost perfectly round in cross section.

Bear Grass *(Xerophyllum tenax)* Pacific Northwest

This plant should not be confused with the Arizona Bear Grass, as addressed in the preceding section. In the Pacific Northwest, Bear Grass is an important pattern material in twined works. It generally grows along dry inland hillsides from Monterey County, California, northward, and in the Sierra Nevada range from about Placer County northward. The inside leaves are used extensively as a weft, rarely, if ever, as a warp and never in a foundation. This Bear Grass is most frequently used as an overlay material in twined ware, or as a false embroidery material, or even as a wrapping material on cradle frames. It is even braided or twisted into coils, dangles, or tassels. When located in the wild, Bear Grass somewhat resembles a cross between a miniature Yucca and a soft lily, as shown in Figures 6 and 7.

Figure 6. Bear Grass on a hillside in Siskiyou County, California.

If Bear Grass isn't burned periodically, it attains a height of maybe twelve inches, at the most, with a rosette display of long slender leaves. However, most basket weavers try to have the plant burned yearly, which forces long healthy leaves in great abundance. It is customarily harvested by "plucking" the central soft, pliable, immature leaves, which are allowed to dry out, causing them to turn a soft ivory-white. However, with age, the white darkens to a rich, glossy, tan color. Figure 7 illustrates a Bear Grass plant that was burned the previous year. Note the rosette of leaves which are long and slender.

*Figure 7. A Bear Grass plant near the Klamath River in
Siskiyou County, California. Note the rosette of leaves,
the innermost of which are harvested.*

Pacific Northwest Bear Grass is easily recognized in a
basket by its honey-tan sheen, or, if recently woven, it may
even have an ivory-white luster. Its flattened appearance, its
high gloss surface, and its striated crepe-paper like texture
are sure signs of Bear Grass. In Puget Sound it is often
dyed vivid colors by the Quinault, the Quileute, Makah/
Nootka, or coastal Salish weavers. However, in northern
California, Bear Grass is rarely, if ever, dyed. Unlike Arizona
Bear Grass, which is used as a foundation material, Pacific
Northwest Bear Grass is used almost exclusively as a
pattern material. Figure 8 is a view of Bear Grass as it may
be found in a northwestern California basket, in this case a
semi-openwork Hupa basket. In most cases Bear Grass is
associated with Maidenhair fern as a pattern element, often
with Hazel warps.

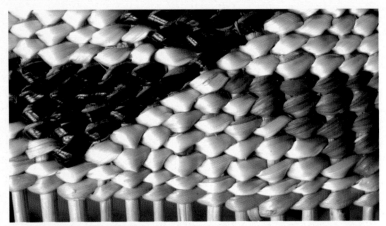

Figure 8. A detail view of Bear Grass as an overlay onto a Spruce root weft, which is hidden on the outer side but visible on the lower whorl and interior. The warps ("sticks") are Hazel shoots, and the dark material is Maidenhair fern.

Bracken fern root *(Pteridium sp.)*

There must be half-a-jillion species of ferns native to California, some growing from a rhizome, a single root, clinging to a rock, or even climbing a tree. The Bracken fern considered here is sometimes referred to as a Brake and is widely distribute from the Mexican border almost to the North Pole. It prefers a reasonable amount of rainfall so don't look for it in Death Valley. Figures 9 and 10 show Bracken ferns in the late autumn in Yosemite Valley, California.

Figure 9. Bracken ferns going dormant in the late autumn in Yosemite National Park.

The ferns shown in Figure 9 are almost completely dormant, which explains why they look dead. Those in the foreground still have some amount of green but will die back in a matter of days, or perhaps a week. This is in contrast to the ferns in Figure 10, which are still quite lively, albeit they will also die back within a short time period. Both photos were taken in Yosemite National Park within approximately one hour of each other. Although these ferns go dormant in the early autumn, the root (rhizome) is still alive and will sprout again next spring. Many basket weavers gather the root during its dormant stage. During its growing season the rhizomes tips are rather fleshy and the internal fiber has not hardened to a usable state.

Figure 10. Bracken Fern fronds
(leaves) while still growing, in Yosemite Valley.

Bracken fern grows from an almost horizontal rhizome about 6" (+/-) below the surface. The rhizome, when first separated from its mother plant, is flattish, knobby, crooked, about the diameter of the little pinky on a pre-teenager, and is harvested by lifting with a digging stick, or a shovel. Its outer coating has a thick, brownish black, mucous-like layer which covers the inner woody material, which also has a coating of more mucous-like stuff about the consistency of week-old sun dried Jell-O. Once this inner mucous material is scraped-wiped-washed away, the rough, flattish, crooked, knobby, brownish, woody material, with many "dog legs" is split longitudinally into two flat pieces, from which two brown, rough, crepe paper-like weaver strands are extracted. When fresh and undyed, these weaver strands are brownish-black, but are almost always dyed black.

When found in a basket, Bracken fern root resembles a cross between a piece of raw hide and a piece of black second-hand crepe paper. The novice (as well as the author) often finds it hard to identify Bracken fern root in a basket because it sometimes closely resembles Devil's Claw. The primary difference between the two is that Devil's Claw is noticeably thick, striated, and may be somewhat striped and faded, while Bracken Fern root is quite thin, and may be deep brown, but generally black, with only tiny striations. When viewed with your trusty $4.98 magnifier, it may even resemble a slightly quilted surface. Devil's Claw is to be discussed later in more detail, but for comparison purposes, it has a tendency to fade in the direct sun and leave a surface of pronounced black and gray streaks, while Bracken fern, which is dyed black, is more densely packed, and, although there are striations, they tend to be almost cellular and uniformly black.

Bracken fern root, as it is used for pattern material, is pictured in a miniature burden basket in Figure 11. This particular basket is a fine miniature northern Paiute burden basket from the Mono Lake region in eastern California, east of the Sierra Nevada range and south of Reno, Nevada. It was purchased at a yard sale together with five other American Indian baskets (six in total) for the ripe old sum of $4.75, total. The author very generously tipped the seller $0.25 to make it an even $5 for six baskets! It pays to shop around!

Paiute people are commonly thought of as being on the western fringe of the Great Basin. The weaving style is primarily diagonal twining with Willow warps and wefts, plus "Sunburned Willow" and Bracken fern root for pattern motifs.

Figure 11. A detailed view of Bracken Fern root in a Paiute basket. Note the striated/cellular texture when greatly magnified. The tan material is Willow.

Because of their relative thinness, some Bracken fern root tends to slightly curl up at the side. Note also the crepe paper-like texture with tiny striations.

Figure 12. Details of Bracken Fern root (black) as a pattern element, associated with "Sunburned Willow" (red) and Willow in a Mono Lake Paiute basket.

Regarding its association with "Sunburned Willow," Figure 12 shows both materials. That material will be discussed in more detail in a later chapter. However, the association of Bracken Fern root with "Sunburned Willow" is almost a sure give-away that the basket originated amongst the northern Paiutes in eastern California or western Nevada.

When viewed with the naked eye, Bracken Fern root appears to be rather dull but of a uniform texture. However, with a magnifier, the black surface may be slightly fibrous with a somewhat quilted surface, and may even have a slightly oily texture, as contrasted with Devil's Claw, which is more deeply striated.

Bulrush Root *(Scirpus spp.)*, a.k.a Tule root

When speaking of this plant; i.e., *Scirpus spp.*, it is generally referred to as "Bulrush" if the discussion revolves about the root, but it is also known as "Tule" if only the upper part of the plant is used for the body of a basket, a mat, or a cradle. Figure 13 depicts Tules on the edge of a lake in Santa Barbara, California. Tules, as a plant material, will be discussed later. For our discussion at this point, Bulrush is described as the root of a Tule plant, as contrasted with Tule as a plant fiber.

Figure 13. Tule (Bulrush plants) on the edge of a lake in Santa Barbara, California.

Use of Bulrush root presumably was reasonably widespread, but not overly common throughout most of western North America. Both Jepson and Moerman list a wide geographical range and an even wider number of varieties of the parent plant, which suggests that Bulrush root may also have been quite widespread, but probably is (was) unrecognized as a basketry plant material. In fact, the author has buttonholed as number of basketry experts and has had poor success finding an "expert" who is really conversant with Bulrush root in an Indian basket.

George Wharton James, in his book *Through Ramona's Country*, made reference to a purple dye for basketry materials using Bulrush root. A basket, formerly collected by George Wharton James, with that alleged purple dye was "owned" by the author a number of years ago but was transferred to the Pechanga tribe in Riverside County, California, circa 2003. Unfortunately, the purple is apparently not a permanent dye in that it had faded to a sort-of gray color.

Figure 14. Natural Bulrush root in a Panamint basket.

Bulrush root, as a weaving material, is harvested from small hair-roots covering large obese rhizomes. When natural; i.e., not dyed, these roots are maroonish-reddish-brownish-black, as shown in Figure 14. When dyed black, Bulrush root is not an uncommon pattern material, most often in coiled baskets.

Bulrush root is easily recognized by its slender, roundish, deeply striated surface; i.e., with perhaps a half dozen longitudinal ridges/grooves, and a tendency to be slightly maroonish-red. If viewed in a basket, using your trusty magnifier, it is quite easy to identify, although it may resemble deeply grooved, dark Yucca root. Because the root is quite small in diameter, and because it is split into two rather than three longitudinal segments, it gives the impression that it represents 180 degrees in cross section rather than being flat, or nearly so.

If you, as a reasonably inexperienced basketry nut, ask around at basket dealers and collectors, looking for Bulrush root in a basket, the chances are 99 out of every 88 times you will get a slightly bewildered look and a response something like *"huh?"* That is because most dealers and many basketry students have seen the material many times but never took the trouble to find out what it is. Of all the persons consulted during this study, Brian Bibby and Bob Hickman, both of Sacramento, are some of the few who were able to recognize the material. At one of Kim Martindale's Indian basketry and art shows in Marin County, California, virtually every dealer present was asked (by me) about Bulrush root, and not one, I repeat not one, could point out the material, even if they were displaying one or more baskets containing the material.

Because of limited recognition of Bulrush root by dealers and collectors, the author has not provided any definitive statements regarding a territorial range for the material. However, when found in a coiled basket, it may be fairly safe to say that the basket originated in the western edge of the Great Basin or Colorado River basin, or in northern California perhaps!

Cattail *(Typha latifolia)*
Before going into any detail regarding Cattails, an

obvious fact should be pointed out that Cattails and Tules are two entirely different plants, albeit they may grow in close proximity to one another, and frequently the layman uses the two terms interchangeably, as though they are the same plant.

They aren't!

Although Cattails were used extensively for all sorts of utilitarian implements throughout North America, both by Indians and by White Guys, the plant is not commonly used for basketry arts. The most usable part of the plant is its leaves, which, being several feet long, were often twisted into a form of cordage, rather than as a solid woody weaver strand such as Hazel, or Red Bud. The most notable exceptions to the above are those baskets created by the Modoc and Klamath people in northeastern California and southeastern Oregon; i.e., in Captain Jack's country.

Figure 15. Cattail plants at a lake in Santa Barbara, California. Early in the season, light brown fruiting "spikes" provided pollen when they start forming, and mature into cottony down-like material. On first glance, Cattail plants somewhat resemble Tules (see Figure 13).

Cattail plants are found most often in, or very near, open water as seen in Figure 15. Their leaves are long and fibrous, almost like shredded palm leaves, and were commonly split into long thin strips which were twisted into cord-like twine, which was then used as wefts in Modoc or Klamath baskets. The Modoc and Klamath people also used split Tule stalk as both warps and wefts in their twined basketry. Brian Bibby states that twisted Cattail leaves appear in a basket as brownish tan, coarse fibers, while split Tule stalks resemble old, dirty Bear Grass. When viewed with the naked eye, Cattail seems to be rather dull and quite coarsely fibrous, as contrasted to Tule which has a dark creamy tan luster like well used Bear Grass.

Without use of your magnifier, Cattail in a twined basket may look somewhat like a poor grade of twisted dark butcher paper. Twisted Cattail wefts may also remind you of a tiny plug of tobacco for giant termites. Now maybe you are not familiar with termite tobacco but this author has been around the block, several times, and has chewed with the best of them!

Figure 16. Twisted Cattail leaves in a mini Modoc cradle .

Inasmuch as Cattail is a rather poor grade of basketry material and cannot withstand very much usage, it was not commonly used in basketry or in creating cradle boards, except in those geographic areas where suitable alternatives were not available, such as in northeastern California (Modoc County) and southeastern Oregon (Klamath County). In some regions, Cattail was used as cordage for household uses, or to tie bunches of whole Tules together for creating water craft. When gathering Cattails for this work, they were harvested while the leaf was still green. Twisting dry leaves would result in crumbling of the fibers. Tules, on the other hand were harvested when dry, when it splits more easily. Note that Cattail leaves, when twisted, show the longitudinal striations which might be compared to fibers in coarse string.

Cedar *(Chamaecyparis lawsoniana)*, Port Orford Cedar

The term "Cedar" is used frequently, and differently, depending upon how far north, or south, or east, or even how far west you are from here. In Arizona and New Mexico, Junipers are referred to as Cedars (which they aren't). In southern California Incense Cedars are called Cedar (which they aren't). In northern California people call Port Orford Cedars a Cedar, (which they aren't). In Washington and British Columbia people refer to a number of cypress-like trees as Cedar (which they also aren't). It fact, Cedar names are about as common in western North America as are Democrats in Chicago.

For our purposes the term "Cedar" is used to describe that basketry material mostly from the Port Orford Cedar *(Chamaecyparis lawsoniana)* or the Western Red Cedar *(Thuja plicata)* of the Pacific Northwest, unless we are talking about northern California, where most of the Cedar is actually Cedar root, and often comes from the Incense Cedar *(Calocedrus decurrens)*.

Because of the great number of trees alluded to as "Cedars," no photographs will be shown of the pseudo-cedar trees that are actually used in creating a Cedar root, or Cedar bark basket. Most trees that Indian basket weavers consider to be Cedars have a rather thick, fibrous, deeply grooved, coarse outer bark, and a much thinner inner bark (phloem), which is composed of numerous paper-thin layers. The latter are harvested by stripping off slabs of this thick outer bark, which also includes the thin inner bark. These slabs may be six to ten feet long, when taken from an old tree trunk, or narrower and thinner on tree limbs. Thin pieces, perhaps 1/2 inch or more wide, and about 1/16 to 1/8 inch thick are carefully separated from the outer bark and trimmed to a workable width before being split into the desired thinness. The resulting strip is about the thickness (or thinness) of ten one dollar bills pressed together.

This inner bark has a noticeable sheen and if it doesn't, it was burnished until it does. In the Pacific Northwest and inland Salish country, strips up to 1/2 inch wide x 1/32 inch thick were often plaited to form the flat base of twined baskets, as shown in Figure 17.

Figure 17. Plaited Cedar bark as used in the base of a Tsimshian basket from the author's collection. Note the high sheen and striations. Note also the flat splints on the base are split into flat warps that proceed up the basket's side.

In many twined baskets from the Pacific Northwest, particularly Washington and British Columbia, the wide Cedar splints from the basket's base were split into thin, narrow strips, then bent upward and used as warps. This is visible in Figure 17 where the flat plaited elements in the upper center are split into two rather wide warps and bent upward, after which they are used in plain twining. Because the warps are so thin, the basket tends to be rather flexible.

Makah and Nootka weavers from the Puget Sound region of Washington, USA, and Vancouver, B.C., also used Cedar bark to form a horizontal basketry rim, which is both ornamental as well as adding to the basket's strength. Such a rim is shown in Figure 18.

Figure 18. Cedar splints used as vertical warps and a horizontal Cedar rim-splint in a Makah basket. The vertical warps near the bottom of the photo are covered by false embroidery of Bear Grass.

Note that in Figure 18, there is a row of Bear Grass at the lower edge of the photo, and the selvage (edge of the rim) has a form of whip stitch of Cedar bark.

Coastal Canadian people, the Kwakiutl, Tsimshian, and Bella Coola people on the Pacific coast south of Alaska, used Cedar very extensively in their *In-Between* weaves. Fig. 19 illustrates Cedar bark in a Tsimshian *In-Between* basket.

*Figure 19. In-Between weaving in a Tsimshian basket.
The warps are Cedar splints. The wide wefts are untwisted
Cedar plaiting, while the whorls between the plaited
rows are plain "Z" twined Cedar.*

Occasionally dyed Bear Grass may wrap the twisted
(twined) weft to create a false embroidery pattern. However,
because the *In-Between* weft is so wide, such false embroidery
is not overly effective. Figure 20 is a detail of red dyed Bear
Grass used as false embroidery on the lid of a Tsimshian In-
Between basket. Note that the Bear Grass wraps the plain
twined weft, not the *In-Between* simple plaited weft. The
reason is rather obvious; i.e., if the false embroidery was
used on the simple plaiting, the colored element would be
too long. Incidentally, the false embroidery on this basket
uses an "S" twist, as contrasted to a "Z" twist in Figure 19.
To see the difference, turn the basket sideways, either left
or right, and the Bear Grass stitch slant is *down-to-the-
right*, as is the case in the letter S. If Z twining had been
used, the Bear Grass stitch would have been *down-to-the-
left*, as is the case in the letter Z.

Figure 20. Details of In-Between weaving showing "S" style false embroidery of red dyed Bear Grass, as contrasted to the "Z" Cedar twining Figure 19.

Twined Cedar bark was used extensively by the British Columbia and Alaskan natives for hats which were quite commonly used for 1) utility purposes, 2) to denote social standing, 3) for whaling expeditions, and 4) to indicate the number of potlatches attended. Although hats are not the subject of this treatise, they present a very fertile topic for a future study.

Chaparral *(Ceanothus cuneatus.)*, Buck Brush, Deer Brush, Wild Lilac, Wait-a-bit Brush, etc.

The word chaparral is an American word, translated from the Spanish, which is often used to describe a patch of hillside brush that rips your Levis, tears up your boots, and gives your horse fits... unless you use tapaderos and chaps, which helps you but not the horse. For those of you unfamiliar with tapaderos, they are heavy pointed leather covering of a saddle's stirrups to protect the rider's boots, but not the horse. Chaps is a corruption of a Spanish word that translates into a leather covering to protect a person's pant legs, but not the horse. To the Indian basket weaver, Chaparral means a very specific plant which we call "Buck Brush", "Wild Lilac", or "Wait a-Bit Brush." The botanical term for this species is Ceanothus *(C. cuneatus)*. The reference to "Buck" comes from the fact that this bush is fed upon quite heavily by deer. Rarely does one find a limb more than several feet long that has not had the tips bitten off. Few shoots are suitable for basketry use, but when suitable shoots are found, Chaparral is preferred over peeled Red Bud or Sumac because it is so tough and durable.

In the central Sierra Nevada region; i.e., Miwok and Sierra (Western) Mono country, Chaparral is often used to construct cradle board vertical elements (a.k.a. "sticks") and face protectors (a.k.a sun shades or visors). When found in a basket or cradle, chaparral is almost indistinguishable from peeled Sumac or even peeled Willow. Its primary difference is that there are numerous buds which often create a jagged spot when the bark is removed. Also, buds are often opposite each other which results in a knobby joint. Figure 21 illustrates a Chaparral plant behind the

Figure 21. A Chaparral (Ceanothus) *bush on a hill behind the Sierra Mono Indian Museum near North Fork, south of Yosemite, California.*

Sierra Mono Indian Museum in North Fork (California). Although not readily visible in the photograph, limbs, or shoots, are quite short and, although they may be relatively straight, they contain numerous buds and twigs, which detract from their quality.

Inasmuch as Chaparral is used almost exclusively in cradle construction, there is no requirement that really long, twig-less shoots be utilized, as is the case in a coiled basket. It is also quite acceptable if there are obvious bud scars in the shoots, provided they are used in the back frame of a cradle. However, Chaparral shoots are used very extensively in the face protector (visor) of Sierra (Western) Mono cradles. Because these face protectors are often bent into a rather tight loop, bud scars of any appreciable size are detrimental, not to the strength but to the bendability of the shoot. Note in Figure 22 that bud scars on a vertical stick are evident in a cradle constructed by Michelle Smith of the North Fork (California) Rancheria.

Figure 22. Chaparral "sticks" in a 2008 Western Mono cradle by Michelle Smith of the North Fork Rancheria in central California. Note the bud scar in the third stick from the right.

In most cases, peeled Chaparral is quite easily confused with peeled Red Bud or Peeled Sumac. In almost all cases, Chaparral is used in conjunction with Red Bud and Sumac, but almost always in a cradle board, not a conventional basket. If the object under consideration is a cradle from the Miwok, Sierra Mono, or Chuckchansi regions of central California, and if the sticks are a honey-tan color, and if the material being inspected has buds that resemble two little eyes and a nose, the chances are better than even money that the material is Chaparral.

Choke Cherry *(prunus spp.)*

Wild (Choke) Cherries may be found growing almost anywhere in the mountains of western America, generally above the 3,000 foot elevation. Unless the soil is fertile and well watered, Choke Cherry plants resemble a short straggly bush. However, if soil conditions are favorable, the plant may reach ten to fifteen feet tall with long, slender, vertical limbs. The plant shown in Figure 23 has shoots reaching ten to twelve feet tall.

Figure 23. Choke Cherry plants, along Hwy 243 in Riverside County, southern California.

The name "choke" didn't come about by accident. You see, Indian folks had (have) the patience of Job and will wait until the fruit is beyond the "fully ripe" stage before tasting it. After the cherry reaches "fully ripe," and if the birds don't get to them first, they dry up, almost like a prune. At this point in their young career they are so good it makes mothers slap their own kids away from the table. The fruit, which resembles tiny Bing cherries, is borne in bunches similar to a loose bunch of grapes, as shown in Figure 24.

Figure 24. Ripe Choke Cherries in Riverside County, California. The fruit is almost black when fully-ripe but dries up like a prune soon thereafter.

The small slender limbs were used, generally unpeeled, for twined utility basketry, and larger limbs were bent into loops for acorn stirrers (hot rock lifters). Unfortunately, when the plant has ideal growing conditions, shoots grow into fat limbs too quickly and it is hard to find small, slender, but long, shoots.

Only a limited number of Indian weavers use(d) Choke Cherry in their basketry. However, some Sierra Mono and some Mono Lake Paiutes, such as Lucy Parker and her mother Dr. Julia Parker, use the slender shoots in making utility baskets. Dr. Julia Parker is actually Pomo, but her husband is Paiute, so Lucy, her daughter is Pomo/Paiute but lives in Mono Lake Paiute territory in California. When used in a utility basket, the unsplit shoot is dark reddish brown in color, as seen in Figure 25.

Figure 25. Choke Cherry in a Lucy Parker basket, commissioned by the author in 2006.

Choke Cherry shoots have bark which is reddish brown and rough with numerous small lenticels and rather deep longitudinal ridges or striations that resemble a tiny, shriveled up salami for Mediterranean midgets. The reddish brown color does not appear until after the first good frost. For utility or novelty baskets, the shoot is used whole. If it is split or peeled, most basketry nuts cannot recognize it as being Choke Cherry except, perhaps by the strong pungent odor it exudes soon after harvesting. Because of the rough texture of the bark, and because it is in a "utility" vessel, most weavers did not place a pattern on their works. Note the small light-colored lenticels in Figure 25.

Conifer Root, Various species

Before starting a discussion of conifer root, it might be well to explain that the word "conifer" should refer to a form of evergreen tree that bears a seed cone.

Jepson says that all conifers belong to the class Gymnospermae, which class includes Pine, Hemlock, Spruce, Fir, Redwood, Cypress, Cedar, Juniper, and even the Yew. Experimentation by your author reveals that roots of one conifer are not appreciably different from those of another conifer; i.e., the interior of a Pine root is not a whole lot different from the root of a Fir tree.

Inasmuch as Indian basket makers, many moons ago, found that roots from certain trees make great basketry materials, they utilized them, but only when appearance was of a secondary consideration, or when other more superior materials were fenced off with no trespassing signs, or when shotgun muzzles subtly suggested that harvesting areas might be more productive elsewhere. The root size most commonly sought after is about the diameter of your thumb, or perhaps your big toe. The roots, were cut into three to four foot long chunks, then either roasted over live coals or buried and baked for several days in a fire pit, or perhaps even boiled, after which the roots were easily split into thin sections and trimmed down to weaver strands. Baking softens the wood fibers and allows the root's bark to be easily removed. If roasted over open coals, the sap sizzles, steams, and boils up, loosening the bark and plant fibers.

Because the parent tree was a conifer, and, because the root came from a conifer tree, it didn't take a rocket scientist to figure out how the term Conifer root came about. Therefore, the term conifer includes a whole genre of basketry plants. The exact species used in a given region varies about as widely as do zeros in the national debt figure.

The two roots shown in Figure 26 are from a Ponderosa Pine tree which the author came into contact with in the northern Sierra Nevada mountains north of Lake Tahoe, and are somewhat typical of most conifers. They started out about the diameter of the author's accusing finger. The bark was removed by holding them over a Coleman stove. The upper root was then split into thirds much as is Sumac or Willow shoots, while the lower root is unsplit.

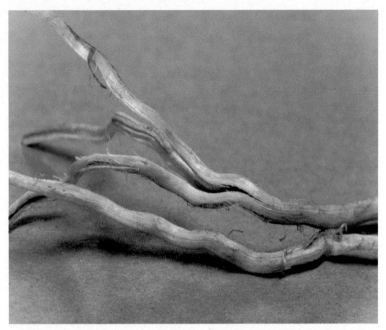

Figure 26. Two Ponderosa Pine roots, the upper one being split into weaver strands while the lower one remains whole.

Roots from Cedar or Fir are not appreciably different from that of this Pine. Baskets may even contain above-ground shoots of Gray Pine (*Pinus sabiniana,* formerly known as "Digger" Pine), which do not look much different from conifer roots. The primary physical difference in pine shoots is that they contain much resin (sap) which can be smelled or felt, while non-pine roots have little such sap. Once incorporated into a basket or cradle, it is almost impossible to distinguish roots of one conifer species from another, unless you coincidentally happen to be brilliant, or have access to a magnifier. No effort will be made to differentiate between roots of any of the conifer trees. Roots used in the Wintu cradle board pictured in Figure 27 are believed to be Pine, probably *Pinus sabiniana,* because many of the other conifers are poorly represented in the Wintu region. Western Yellow pine (*P. ponderosa*) can be found in portions of Wintu country, so it is possible the material in Figure 27 may be Ponderosa pine.

Figure 27. Conifer root as used in a Wintu mini cradle.

When found in an Indian basket or cradle board, Conifer root will, in almost every case, be confined to either northern California or western Oregon and Washington. True, conifers grow in southern California and throughout the Southwest. However, they were normally not used in those areas for basketry.

In a northern California basket, or one from the Pacific Northwest, Conifer root can be recognized by the rather coarse, fibrous, waxy, slightly oily, uneven surface, as seen in Figure 27. When viewed with a 7X, or greater, magnifier, the root has a mass of tiny fibers, or open pores, which carried the sap from the roots to the leaves. These fibers shrivel up when dry and may even resemble Cedar bark. However, when not greatly magnified, the surface appears to be rather coarse. Note that this coarse texture does not lend itself very well toward a finely woven basket.

Cottonwood *(Populus fremontii)*

Although Cottonwood was rarely used as a basketry material in coastal or mountainous California or the Pacific Northwest, it does appear occasionally in basketry of the

Colorado River basin, and occasionally in cradles by the Foothill Yokuts people of California. Inasmuch as it was not a commonly used basketry material, it will be touched upon rather briefly herein.

A conventional basket composed of Cottonwood shoots is about as scarce as money in your son's checking account. This apparent hiatus is probably due to the fact that Cottonwood is not easily recognized in a basket. But, like the flu bug, it may be all around a person but not recognized. When found in a basket, or cradle, Cottonwood is often hard to tell from Willow, Chaparral, or peeled Red Bud. If the basketry item is reasonably fresh, Cottonwood is almost snow white with a noticeable cottony texture with no striations.

Figures 28 and 29 show a Cottonwood tree as fairly small. However, in Desert washes, where water is near the surface, Cottonwood trees can reach a trunk diamiter of six feet, or more. Heights of fifty feet, or more, are not uncommon.

Figure 28. A small Cottonwood tree in Riverside County, So. California.

Figure 29. Cottonwood leaves and shoots.

Figure 30 depicts Cottonwood weaver strands just prior to being used in a basket. Of particular interest is how the

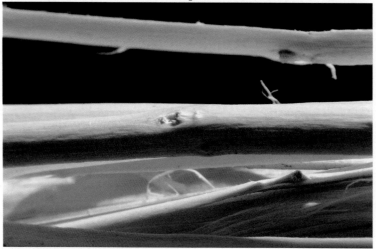

Figure 30. Details of Cottonwood weaver strands prior to being used in a basket. Note the tiny bud scars which often protrude out as in the middle shoot.

bud scar protrudes out, not unlike tiny volcanoes (sans eruptions) rather than being recessed. Inasmuch as there are numerous leaves on a Cottonwood shoot, there are numerous buds.

When fresh, Cottonwood has virtually no surface features, such as striations, or waxy surface, or wrinkles. However, as it ages, the whiteness darkens to a pale but lusterless honey-tan hue, and the cotton-like surface gives way to a smooth but dull texture, not unlike Willow. Even with advanced age there are few striations and little, if any, luster or patina. It is in these latter stages that Willow and Cottonwood become very similar in appearance.

Deer Grass *(Muhlenbergia rigins)*, Clump Grass, Bunch Grass, etc.

Deer Grass is almost as ubiquitous as people in a hospital emergency room on Saturday night. It is (was) used very extensively throughout much of southern and central California and portions of the Southwest as a foundation material for coiled basketry.

Inasmuch as we are talking about foundation material, let's talk about basket making techniques. For those who are beginners in Indian basketry, there are several basic styles of basket making in western North America; i.e., coiling, twining, and plaiting. Only the coiling method uses a foundation material. In this style, which we are concerned with at this point, a bundle of material, the foundation, is gathered together, much like fibers in a rope or an electrical cable, and wrapped with a weaver strand. In southern and central California, Deer Grass seed stalks are the most commonly used foundation material, albeit some southern California basket makers used scrap Juncus, or even whole Juncus rods, as did the Chumash and Gabrielino weavers.

Deer Grass is a perennial plant that resembles a pint sized Pampas Grass, with its tall emerging seed stalk. Deer Grass plants prefer a moist soil, although they can be found growing on a bare hillside, as seen in Figure 31. The usable portion of the plant is actually the seed stalk, which forms in mid summer and matures in the late autumn, after it achieves three to four feet in length. The leaves are never used. The seed stalk is normally hollow and is covered with tiny seeds throughout the upper portion, kind of like bristles on a skinny bottle brush. These seeds are exceedingly tiny but terribly onerous if they penetrate your skin, which they often do.

Figure 31. Deer Grass on a sidehill near Highway 49 in Tuolumne County, California. Note the slight spring, or seepage.

The seeds, which are barely visible in Figure 32, are so small it is almost impossible to extract them from your skin. Consequently they must be stripped from the stalk before use. Some weavers pull the stalk between two dry corn cobs which removes not only the seeds but also the tiny stems holding the seeds.

Deer Grass seed stalks are used extensively throughout southern and central California, and for some basketry in the Southwest. They are used because of their stiffness, their rigidity, and availability. Figure 32 shows a mature plant with seed stalks three to four feet long. Much of what is visible is really leaves, which droop over near the ground. Note that the upper 2/3rds of the seed stalk is covered with tiny seeds which are barely visible, until they penetrate your skin, when they become very obvious. These seed are customarily stripped off prior to being used in a basket.

Figure 32. A closer view of
Deer Grass showing very slender seed stalks.

Although Yucca leaf fibers are the most common "start" material for coiled basketry in southern California, some basket makers create their "starts" by wadding up the tips of Deer Grass stalks and then piercing this wad with the weaver strand, much like you would pierce a voodoo doll of your favorite enemy.

Deer Grass in a foundation is wrapped by weaver strands, often Juncus or Sumac, which hide it from view (most of the time). Figure 33 shows portions of a "Mission" basket in which a Deer Grass foundation is covered by basal red and tan Juncus stitching material. A close inspection of the photo shows evidence of its Deer Grass foundation.

Figure 33. A "Mission" basket in the author's collection.
Look carefully at the Deer Grass foundation material which is
partially exposed. This is a "canoe" shaped basket which explains
the sharp corners, which are not common in most coiled baskets.

In some older baskets, stitches may be missing, particularly on the basket's rim, which exposes the foundation to view, as is the case illustrated in Figure 34, where the bundle of Deer Grass (foundation) has been exposed by the missing stitches.

Deer Grass is easily recognized in these cases by the fact that there are a number of slender stalks, generally approximately 1/16" or less in diameter, composing the foundation's bundle. In the southern portion of the Sierra Nevada mountains, Deer Grass seed stalks may approach 1/8" diameter and may be mistaken for rods. When viewed with a magnifier, these stalks show very tiny longitudinal striations, plus what looks like tiny whiskers. Art Silva, who partnered with the late Bill Cain in basketry classes at several universities in southern California, used to carry a sewing needle with which he would penetrate the foundation materials to see if they are hollow, like Deer Grass, or a solid rod, like Willow or Red Bud. Don't you do that! Some basket owners look with a jaundiced eye on people who poke holes in their basketry materials. It is much wiser to use your magnifier rather than a needle. If you are really lucky, you can find a basket which is shamelessly exposing its foundation, as in Figure 34.

Quite frequently, when Deer Grass is exposed due to

Figure 34. Exposed Deer Grass as a bundle foundation in a "Mission" basket with Sumac stitching.

missing stitches, as in the preceding photo, the Deer Grass seed stalks actually splinter into shreds and appear to be much thinner than they really are.

Devil's Claw (*Martynia proboscidea)*

Rarely will a southern California Indian basket be found containing Devil's Claw, except perhaps (very rarely) in the southeastern corner of San Diego County, and occasionally along the eastern fringes of the Sierra Nevada range. It is, however, used extensively throughout the Southwest.

As a plant (see Figure 35), it is about as welcome to farmers and cattlemen as halitosis. Devil's Claw plants seem to thrive in hot arid conditions, particularly if there is irrigation to boot. In the Sacramento-San Joaquin valleys of California, agricultural agencies, farmers, and cattlemen do all they can to eradicate it. The Tohono O'odham people of southwestern Arizona, however, propagate and cultivate a variety of this plant that grows horns almost as long as those on a Texas Longhorn steer (*well … almost*).

When found growing in the wild, the plant might be

Figure 35. A Devil's Claw plant in bloom and with immature fruit, (center foreground) from the Sacramento Valley.

mistaken for some exotic form of pumpkin or squash. There are attractive bell-like blossoms, and the fruit may remind you of a fuzzy green carrot with tips that curl up like a fish hook. When the fruit matures, the green fuzzy outer rind dries up and peels away, like on a banana, revealing the black harvestable "horns," as shown in Figure 36. After the horns mature, they are deep gray to almost jet black in color, with spikes running down its back, somewhat like a miniature dinosaur, with two eight inch to twelve inch long horns, the tips of which are more pointed than a needle and as strong as a steel spike. They also curve outward and then inward like claws on a lobster.

Figure 36. Three mature Devil's Claw "Horns" in the center of the photo. Immature horns are in lower right, above the lower-right blossom.

To extract a weaver strand, the horn is soaked overnight and a slice is taken from the outside of each horn. Although the horns are black when fresh, they tend to fade if exposed to the direct summer sun. It has been rumored about (unsubstantiated of course) that some Arizona basket makers bake Devil's Claw by roasting it overnight in a fire pit until it is medium-well. These same unsubstantiated sources tell me that baking enhances the black color and keeps it from fading.

To recognize Devil's Claw in a basket, look carefully at the black. If it has a thick, tough, rawhide appearance, as shown in Figure 37, with many longitudinal striations that tend to be black, or gray, and if the material makes you think of a rhinoceros, then it probably is Devil's Claw. If it doesn't have the striations, and reminds you of a soft cuddly baby rhinoceros, it might very well be Bracken fern root.

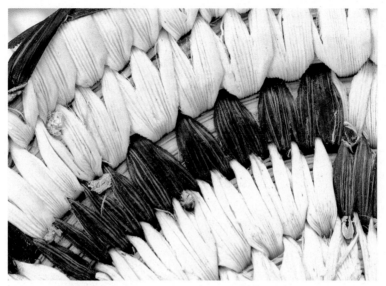

*Figure 37. Devil's Claw in a Tohono O'odham
basket, a gift from Bob Hickman of Old Sacramento.*

Dogwood (*Cornus spp.*), Creek Dogwood

Hickman (*Jepson Manual*, 1993) lists six varieties of
Dogwood native to California, while Moerman lists eighteen
species used by American Indians across this great land of
milk and honey. Margaret (Peg) Mathewson, a friend and
an authority on plants used by Indians, calls the specific
variety to be discussed herein Brown Dogwood (*Cornus
glabrata*), whereas Moerman (pp 177 to 180) lists several
varieties, such as Pacific Dogwood *(C. nautili)* and Red Osier
(*C. sericea* a.k.a. *C. Californica* or *C. stolonifera*), but not *C.
glabrata*, as the dogwood used by California Indians in their
basketry. If the smart money cannot agree on a specific
species, then this country boy is kind of stranded out in
left field. When used as a basketry pattern material, Creek
Dogwood is the only term the author will use.

Based upon the foregoing, it is apparent that authors on
Indian baskets are not necessarily good botanists. This one
(the author, that is,) however can recognize Creek Dogwood
when he finds it is a basket, which is very rarely. Those
baskets he has come across with Creek Dogwood seem to

Figure 38. A Dogwood plant growing along side a highway in Yosemite National Park. The photo was taken in late October.

have originated along the western edge of the Sierra Nevada mountains in central California, primarily with the Sierra Miwok and occasionally with the Maidu and Sierra Mono people. In reading the literature, Dogwood (by whatever botanical name) is mentioned occasionally in California's Northwest, with the Yuki, and Pomo weavers. However, it was not used to any extent even in that region.

In the few cases where Creek Dogwood was used in a basket, it formed an accent material in twined utility baskets where the pinkish purple-red bark was used to accentuate warps in winnowing trays. In those cases the tray contains widely spaced longitudinal warps as an ornamental element.

Creek Dogwood shoots are fairly easy to recognize by their rather waxy surface with numerous tiny splotches of gray which might remind the reader of tiny blisters. The material is gathered in late autumn or winter along creek beds in the Sierra Nevada Mountain Range.

During the growing season, the plant, or perhaps more properly called the shrub, has vivid yellow-green foliage. In the early autumn it is one of the first to change color, the leaves turning a very pleasant pinkish red color, as seen in Figure 38. It is also recognized by its pinkish purple-red bark, and the fact that leaves are widely spaced and opposite each other, plus the tiny blisters.

In most cases the Creek Dogwood warp, is used as an accent element running the length of twined trays. It does not seem to be used for strength, but only for its colored bark. Unfortunately, this vivid bark has a nasty habit of flaking off, exposing the buff underlying cambium layer.

Unfortunately, baskets with Creek Dogwood are almost impossible to acquire. Therefore, the author commissioned such a basket, warps and wefts from which are shown in Figure 39.

Figure 39. Creek Dogwood warps and wefts.
Note the lenticels and the rather waxy surface.

Wild Grape Vine (*Vitis californica*)

Wild grape vines can be found in almost every corner of western North America, except the salt flats of Death Valley or the glaciers of Alaska/Canada. They prefer stream beds or near springs, but are occasionally found on what appears to be dry hillsides (covering a seep or spring), as in Fig. 40.

Figure 40. Grape Vines adjacent to Hwy 49, Mariposa County,
California. Note the vines covering a Cottonwood tree.

The vines themselves are not generally used as weaver warps or wefts. However, some tribes use(d) the long slender vines as ropes or reinforcement hoops about the rim or belly of twined baskets to give them strength. Because this treatise, so far, focuses on weaver strands, warps, and wefts, no detailed photos of grape vine usage in basketry are shown, and the text kind of "waltzes around" the subject of ropes or reinforcing rods. Some of the northern California tribes made extensive use of Grape roots.

Wild Grape root (*Vitis californica*)

Wild grape vines were discussed in the preceding paragraphs. The following pages address Wild Grape roots. Some Klamath River (California) basket makers; i.e., Yurok, Hupa, and Karuk people, use Grape roots extensively in their twined basketry, both as warps and wefts. Wild grapes are prolific along the banks and sandbars of creeks and rivers, where high spring runoff waters wash up large quantities of fine sand. Where vines are dense, there is often a maze of both large "parent" roots and tiny "hair" roots. Figure 41 shows a section of a "parent" root almost one inch thick,

Figure 41. A section of Grape root from the Klamath River in Siskiyou County, California. Note the large "parent" root and several dozen smaller "hair" roots.

plus about two dozen smaller "hair" roots sprouting from the main root. It is these smaller roots that are harvested, peeled, and used as both warps and wefts by these Klamath River Indian basket makers.

Wild grapes are very prolific along stream and creek beds in the Pacific Northwest, and although their roots are reasonably easy to harvest, so also are Willow roots. In fact, Sand Bar Willow roots are even easier to harvest than are paychecks in some cities. As a consequence, many basket makers, particularly along the Klamath River in northern California, seem to prefer Willow root to Grape root, which means Grape root in a basket is not nearly as common as is Willow root. To obtain Grape roots, a person must get down on the "ole prayer bones" in the soft sandy silt bordering a river and dig down perhaps six inches until a maze of hair roots are encountered. Prayer bones is a sage old Indian term which can be translated as a person's "Sunday-go-ta-meet'n knees." Figure 42 shows Verna Reece holding a Grape root whose fleshy outer bark has been stripped away and the inner woody portion split into three segments to be used as wefts.

Figure 42. Verna Reece holding a split Grape root.

Grape root is often hard to recognize in a basket because it closely resembles peeled Willow or Hazel; i.e., it is relatively cottony-smooth but has noticeable longitudinal striations with a slightly chalky dark tan luster. The root Verna Reece gathered in the previous photo is bigger than most Grape roots used by her people. This explains why it was split into thirds and intended as a weft rather than a warp. The bark is stripped off soon after being gathered. Otherwise the woody core turns an undesirable dark color and becomes brittle. When used as an unsplit warp, a slight bulge may occasionally occur where the root tried to branch. This bulge slightly resembles peeled Hazel, sans the "kink." However, when split, this bulge is rarely seen. Figure 43 shows peeled Grape root in a Yurok basket by Lena Hurd. A close look with your trusty $4.98 (plus tax) magnifier will show little difference between Grape root and peeled Willow root.

Figure 43. Grape roots in a Yurok basket by Lena Hurd.

Hazel (*Corylus rostrata*), Wild Hazel Nut, Wild Filbert Nut

Hazel is one of the more commonly used basketry materials throughout northern California and the Pacific

Northwest. The plant is either a short sparse tree or a tall sparse shrub, depending upon soil and environmental conditions. The domesticated plant, which is far less sparse, is a source of commercial filberts, a.k.a. hazel nuts. Figure 44 shows a seven to eight foot tall Hazel "tree" along the highway in Yosemite National Park.

Figure 44. A Hazel bush (tree) along HWY 41 in Yosemite Park. Note its relative size as compared with an adjacent Pine tree.

When viewed by a motorist driving by at 75 MPH, Hazel may not be much different than any other sparse bush which deer use to hide behind. Even when the driver slows down to about 15 MPH, and doesn't get rear-ended, the plant doesn't look like much. However, to an Indian basket maker, this plant offers more potential than does a bale of oat hay to a race horse. One of the most distinguishing aspects of a Hazel bush is the shape of the leaves. Figure 45 shows the crenulated Hazel leaves.

Inasmuch as coiling is not a common weaving technique in northern California, Hazel is found mostly in twined basketry, as well as openwork utility ware and cradles. Hazel shoots are used as warps because of their rigidity yet flexibility and their strength. To the unaided eye, Hazel shoots, when peeled, look somewhat similar to Willow.

Figure 45. Hazel leaves showing the crenulated margins. Note the thin shoots in the upper right and middle right of the photo.

Leaves on a Hazel limb, or shoot, are offset about every six inches, rather than being opposite, as is the case with Dogwood and many other plants. As a consequence, peeled Hazel shoots usually exhibit a slight "kink," or "dog leg" (see Figure 46) which is almost diagnostic for Hazel shoots. To

Figure 46. Hazel as warps in a cradle by Loren Bommelyn, a Yurok man from Crescent City, California. Note the "Hazel kinks".

the uninitiated, this "kink," under a magnifier looks like a tiny nose, a puckered mouth, and two eyes. For purposes of this treatise, this configuration is referred to as a "Hazel Kink." Willow buds, on the other hand, occasionally cause a bud scar, which appears under that trusty magnifier as a recess in the strand but sans the Hazel Kink.

In a few cases, but not many, Hazel is split longitudinally into thin weaver strands and used as wefts in a twined basket or, more rarely, as a wrapping of a cradle frame. However, it is more commonly used unsplit where the weft is not twisted radically, as in the case of the cradle pictured in Figure 47.

When found in a twined basket or cradle, Hazel appears as a slender shoot that was once almost white but soon turned a rich honey-tan. When viewed under magnification, the surface may resemble Willow, sans kinks. In fact most basketry "experts" (including this author) can't tell the difference without seeing the Hazel Kinks. If there is a difference, Willow appears to be very slightly more cottony. Figure 47 shows Hazel in a Crescent City, California, Yurok

Figure 47. Hazel warps and wefts. These wefts are whole; i.e., they are not split. Note the "Hazel Kink" in the weft almost in the center of the photo.

cradle by Loren Bommelyn. In this case, because the warps are widely spaced, Mr. Bommeyln used very thin, unsplit Hazel as wefts. In most baskets, and some cradles, warps (sticks) tend to be rather short. However, in this cradle, Mr. Bommelyn used sticks that, in some cases extend from top to bottom; i.e., about 24 inches long. Most sticks are not that long and are often spliced.

Juncus (*Juncus textilis*), Wire Grass

Perhaps one of the most commonly used basketry plants in southern California is Juncus, a member of the Reed (Rush) family. It has been rumored about (unsubstantiated, of course) that there are fifty (+/-) species or varieties of Juncus growing in California alone, not counting those outside the state, or those I've missed or forgotten. Some are only six inches tall while others may reach twelve feet (144 California inches). Most prefer a damp canyon floor, usually under a canapé of oaks and sycamore trees, as shown in Figure 48.

Figure 48. Juncus in a canyon under a canapé of oaks and sycamores (the light colored trunk on the right,) off Hwy 74, Riverside County, California.

Figure 49. Juncus in an open field near Anza on the Cahuilla Reservation, Riverside County, southern California.

For every statement as positive as on the previous page re canyon floors, there is an equal and opposite statement, such as, "Juncus is often found in open fields," such as the *cienega* shown in Figure 49. *Cienega* is a sage old California Indian word meaning a wet place

Juncus can be found in Indian basketry from the coastal plains of Baja California, up the California coast to, (I forget the place but it's north of Santa Barbara), and then from the Pacific Ocean inland to, (I forget that place too, but it's near the south end of the San Joaquin Valley!). From there Juncus extends inland and south to (I forgot that place also). Eva Slater, who is probably the most knowledgeable person on Panamint and Western Shoshonean baskets this side of Mars explained to the author that the Panamint weavers often used *Juncus cooperii*. Juncus also appears in Chemehuevi and Moapa Paiute basketry. That species appears to be Juncus *textilis*.

Inasmuch as use of Juncus is reasonably widespread, one would think that the same species, or variety, covers a fairly wide region. Not so! It seems that the plant is slightly different every place it grows. I once gathered a nice batch of *Juncus textilis* in northern Santa Barbara County, California, where the reed was almost eight feet tall and as big in diameter as your little pinky (well,... almost!). Yet not more than 200 yards away is another stand of *Juncus textilis* that barely reaches four feet tall and perhaps not half as big as your little pinky. Why you might ask is there that much difference in such a short distance? The answer is, damned if I know, or, as my late departed cousin Dave Osuna, who spoke the Hokan language on the Santa Ysabel Indian Rez, used to say, *k'eeen sa'aabe*! (that's a sage old Indian phrase meaning, "damned if I know").

Juncus is easily recognized in a basket by its smooth, glossy texture and the numerous longitudinal striations, although in an older basket, that gloss may be worn to a dull luster. Figure 50 illustrates both natural tan and basal red Juncus in a "Mission" basket.

When first gathered, Juncus is a deep forest green but when fully mature has a whisper of silvery yellow-blue tint.

If the reed is gathered during the summer, when it is still growing vigorously, the basal six (+/-) inches (the "earth end") is white and rather pulpy. When the reed dries, this pulpy end stays white and may appear so in a finished basket. A close examination with a magnifier will show this white material to be slightly shriveled, as compared with the mature, upper, "sky end".

Figure 50. Natural Tan and Basal red Juncus in a southern California "Mission" basket. Note the mildew spots in those stitches in the middle of the photo.

To bleach out the green in a Juncus reed, the author, who lives in the Los Angeles basin of southern California, places the freshly harvested Juncus on top of his garage roof during the summer months, but takes it in before rain or heavy dew, which happens about once every two or three decades in southern California (we get our rain from the California Aqueduct). If left in the dew or rain, Juncus has a nasty habit of mildewing and in many cases may contain a number of reddish brown blotches, as seen in Figure 50. It does not damage the structure of the material but does detract from its appearance, unless of course, you are looking for that old, antique-look. Exposure to several months of direct sun on a garage roof takes care of the green, leaving a nice sand-tan hue which you expect to see in a "Mission" basket. If Juncus is gathered in the late autumn or winter, the reeds can be placed on the dashboard of a car to protect them from rain or dew but still utilize the sun's rays for bleaching out the green. In this latter case, bleaching may take more than several months, depending upon how much sun versus how much rain you have.

The basal red material at the lower, or earth, end of the reed is, however, colorfast and won't fade after fifty years (+/-) of sunshine. However, it is safer to cover that basal red with a board while it is resting on the garage roof, just to make sure that the red does not lighten a wee bit.

To an experienced "Mission basketry nut," such as a guy who owns and uses a $4.98 (plus tax) magnifier, the length and character of basal red Juncus in a basket offers a clue as to the origin of the basket. Long, deeply hued, basal brick-red Juncus is often associated with San Diego County's Back Country; i.e., the mountainous areas around Julian, Santa Ysabel, or Mesa Grande (southern California). Soil and climatic conditions there tend to produce basal red that can be as long as ten to twelve inches. Normally the basal red is not over six inches long (+/-), nor does it exhibit that deep brick red color elsewhere. This is not to say that other areas do not also produce vivid basal red Juncus ... sometimes!

Parenthetically, the length of a basal red weaver strand can sometimes be estimated by counting the number of stitches with the red color and then applying a rule-of-thumb guide (per Justin Farmer) as follows: In a coiled basket with an average stitch count of ten to twelve stitches per inch, and four to four and one-half coils per inch, a single stitch represents about one inch of original weaver strand. In other words; six to eight stitches of basal red in a basket means the basal red weaver strand was six to eight inches long, plus the length of the bound under fag, plus the unused running end. In Figure 51, there are twelve stitches of basal red Juncus in the middle whorl. A *Bound-Under-Fag-End-Stitch* (BUFES) separates those stitches from eight additional stitches of basal red Juncus, before the Juncus changes to a mild tan. This suggests the first basal red strand was twelve + inches long.

Figure 51. Twelve stitches of basal red Juncus in the middle whorl (row) of a "Mission" basket. Note the use of Bound Under Fag End Stitches (BUFES), a.k.a. "Mission Stitch".

Perhaps the majority of "Mission" baskets contain black Juncus as a pattern material. The proportion of dyed black to basal red or tan Juncus is often used as a clue to the basket's origin. A discussion of Juncus used in a "Mission" basket is included in chapter three, earlier in this treatise.

To achieve a color-fast black dye, some weavers soaked the split and sized weaver strand in a solution of water, old rusty nails, and acorn fragments for several weeks, or more, depending upon the weather. The iron oxide (rust) does the actual dying, and tannin from acorns act as a mordant to set and hold the dye. If the reader plans to try this process, be sure to get the written permission of the lady of the house, the local health department, and the local Air Pollution Control Board first, because the smell, scum, gnats, and insects associated with the process is almost as bad as brewing up sauerkraut. Figure 52 illustrates use of iron dyed Juncus in a Soboba basket.

Figure 52. Dyed black Juncus in a Soboba ("Mission") basket in the author's collection. The tan material is Sumac.

Apparently some pre-contact weavers buried their weaver strands in iron rich mud near a spring or seep, or in the edge of a lake or salt water bay, where certain chemicals or organic matter effectuated the black dye. Other weavers soaked their strands in a solution of Elderberry leaves-flowers-berries, plus some mashed acorns for a mordant, to create a black dye. Once in a blue moon a basketry nut will find a basket in which strands were colored with a red or yellow, or even a blue dye. The red may vary from dark brownish red to almost pink. These colors almost certainly resulted from a commercial (aniline, a.k.a *Rit*) dye. In almost all cases, the presence of a commercial dye is easy to detect because the color is relatively consistent over a length of the pattern, which is unusual for a natural color. Although a yellow dye, such as from Durango root, was reportedly used, the author has only seen traces of yellow in a basket one time, and he has seen Indian baskets numbering well into the many thousands. Blue may possibly be from an indigo dye used for dying cloth. If the reader has a basket with a commercial dyed pattern material, be advised that these colors fade very easily if exposed to direct sunlight, so keep them shaded at all times and minimize their exposure to fluorescent lights.

Inasmuch as basket makers from southern California also used vast amounts of Sumac in their basketry, a logical question might be asked: Did they also dye Sumac?" The answer is, "rarely," because Sumac does not readily accept a dye, be it rusty iron or an aniline dye.

In George Wharton James' book *Through Ramona's Country*, reference is made to a purple dye created by two sisters in northeastern San Diego County. Roots from the Tule plant were allegedly used to create this dye. Very few examples of this material are extant. However, approximately ten years ago the author purchased a basket from Leon Taylor of Fresno, which basket was collected by George Wharton James in the very early 1900s, containing such a dye. Unfortunately the dye was not colorfast and had faded to a dirty gray color. That basket is now in the Justin Farmer Collection on the Pechanga Rez in Riverside County, California. A similarly dyed globular basket was once owned by a gentleman in Julian, southern California. Ironically, the dye on that specific basket applied to both the Sumac and Juncus. The purple dye had not faded unduly from the Sumac but was almost entirely gone from the Juncus. This contradicts the above statement, re Sumac not taking a dye.

Maidenhair Fern *(Adiatum pedatum)*, Five Finger Fern

There must be half a zillion varieties of Maidenhair Fern in nurseries across this land of golden sunshine. Most, if not all, have a long slender stem with a reddish-maroon, almost black, iridescent sheen. The stems on most nursery varieties are upwards of twelve inch long. Although some may be only four inches long and 1/16 of an inch or less in diameter, others' stems may be eighteen inches long and 1/8 of an inch thick. A few are relatively tough, but most tend toward brittleness.

The Five Finger fern, a.k.a Maidenhair fern, which we are addressing here, derives its name from the five compound leaves, somewhat resembling a human hand with its five fingers. There are two plants growing almost side-by-side in Figure 53, plus several lesser plants in the undergrowth.

Note that each plant contains the referenced five fronds (leaves), like your hand, except that the thumb is like that on King Kong (I think). Although not clearly visible in Figure 53, stems on these ferns are almost twenty inches long.

Figure 53. Maidenhair Fern plants, as well as Sedge and a host of other plants in a Siskiyou forest, northern California.

Most Maidenhair fern stems are brightly colored and glossy, but tend to be brighter on one side than on the other; i.e., one side tends toward a lighter reddish brown while the other side is a deeper maroonish red with a noticeable sheen. It is the side with the sheen that most weavers use. Although many Pacific Northwest Indian weavers discard the lighter side and use only the dark sheen side, in a few areas the other side may be saved for those uses where the sheen and deep color are not important.

When found in a Pacific Northwest basket, Maidenhair fern, at a slight distance, appears to be almost black. However, when viewed through a magnifier, the deep maroonish red becomes self evident, as does its smooth polished surface, with what appears to be subsurface longitudinal striations under the smooth surface. When the material is reasonably fresh, Maidenhair fern stems are so glossy one might think they have been varnished. This high luster is presumably why the material is used.

Care must be taken in harvesting the stems as they can be brittle when not handled properly. They tend to dry quite rapidly after being harvested, and unless kept moist they become almost unworkable when dry, or even partially dry.

Figure 54 depicts the use of Maidenhair fern in a Hupa basket, together with Bear Grass as a weft and Alder-dyed Woodwardia as an overlay. Note the luster of both Maidenhair fern and Bear Grass, and the contrast which is achieved by use of the three plant materials. Note also the high luster, or sheen, of the Maidenhair fern, which photographs as bluish black but actually has a very slight maroon hue.

Figure 54. Maidenhair fern stems (bluish black), Bear Grass (white), and Woodwardia (red) in a Hupa basket in the author's collection.

Maple *(Acer macrophylum)*, Big Leaf Maple

Unless a basketry nut is really well read and has peeked into the bowels of at least 1572 (or more) California baskets, the chances are pretty good that discussions re Big Leaf Maple will elicit a comment like ... whaaaaa???

Anyone who has spent more than fifteen minutes in California north of the Mason-Dixon Line (a.k.a. the Tehachapi Mountains) will recognize Big Leaf Maple as a shrubby tree with leaves not unlike those that gladden the hearts of most Canadians. If you happen to be south near Los Angeles, just crank up the old Hupmobile and take an afternoon drive up the Angeles Crest Highway. Once you are above the scrub brush and into the trees, you'll find Big Leaf Maple in every canyon (almost!). If you happen to be in the San Bernardino Mountains (Los Angeles County) Maple trees out number politicians three to one.

The tree shown in Figure 55 is growing along the aforementioned Angeles Crest Highway above the town of La Canada north of Los Angeles. This tree stands about 15

Figure 55. A Big Leaf Maple tree growing along side the Angeles Crest Highway immediately north of Los Angeles.

feet above the ground but a mile below the sky, which is about par for Big Leaf Maple in southern California.

In northern California or the Pacific Northwest, trees get quite a bit bigger. The photo in Figure 56 shows maple leaves on a tree along the Klamath River Highway, just as they start turning yellow in early October. Leaves in southern California do not turn the vivid yellow that one sees to the north.

Figure 56. Big Leaf Maple leaves turning yellow in early October, Siskiyou County, California.

Unfortunately there is little reliable information as to which weavers used Big Leaf Maple, although many self proclaimed experts claim that it was (is) used quite extensively. When peeled, split and sized as a weaver strand in a coiled basket, it is hard to recognize once it gets into a basket, albeit the material is similar to peeled Red Bud or even Sumac. Those basketry experts who are much wiser than me, claim that Big Leaf Maple, when first used in a basket, is not unlike peeled Red Bud. However, within a reasonably short time Maple turns a rich honey-tan color, as shown in the photograph in Figure 57.

Figure 57 depicts Big Leaf Maple in a Maidu basket. Note that it has turned a honey-tan color and is accompanied by Red Bud pattern material.

Figure 57. Big Leaf Maple in a Mountain Maidu basket in the author's collection. Note the use of Red Bud for a pattern element.

Parenthetically, the basket photographed in Figure 57 is of the coiled technique, which is just about the northern limit of coiling in California. True, the Pomos and the Yukis used coiling for some of their baskets, but, in general, twining is the more common technique in northern California.

Milk Weed (*Asclepia spp.*), fibers only

Although this jumble of words deals mostly with plants used to create basketry or cradles, several plant species are included, from which outer bark was used to create fibers ancillary to basket or cradle making. Milk Weed is one of those plants. Rarely was it used as either a warp or a weft, but it was used occasionally as a "start" in coiled basketry or as cordage in cradles. With the possible exception of

Indian Hemp, Milk Weed fibers are generally considered to be the strongest, and perhaps the most attractive, of all native fibers. When thoroughly cleaned, the fibers are very silky and almost transparent, like mono-filament fishing line. Although commonly used as a cordage fiber, it was rarely used as a weaving fiber.

Figure 58. A Milk Weed plant growing on the Yosemite Valley floor. See also Figure 59. Both photos were taken the same day.

There are several species, or varieties, of Milk Weed growing throughout western North America. The species shown in Figures 58 and 59 is the one most often used in southern California.

The above photo in Figure 58, and that in Figure 59, were taken in Yosemite Valley on October 10, within an hour of each other. One plant (Figure 58) is still growing, while the other plant (Figure 59) has matured and expired (above ground). Please note the matured and opened seed pod in the center of Figure 59. Each seed has a silky fleece which blows in the wind as does down from a thistle.

*Figure 59. A Milk Weed plant which has expired for the season.
Both this and the previous photo were taken the same day.*

When mature, these plants may stand twenty-four to thirty inches tall and die back after bearing their seed crop. The rhizome, from which the stalk emerges in the spring, does not die, however.

To obtain Milk Weed fibers, the papery thin outer skin is either stripped or washed away from its inner bark, revealing tiny silken fibers which are almost as transparent as a fishing line, but are exceedingly strong, almost like silk. If the purpose is to use only the silken fibers, the gray outer bark is washed away from the fibers, either before or after being stripped from the stalk. However, for most purposes, that gray matter does not adversely impact the fibers which are then twisted into cordage much as are fibers of Agave, Yucca, or Nettle.

Figure 60 illustrates a Milk Weed stalk ready for processing, with the outer bark in the process of being stripped away and ready to be converted to cordage. Note the dry, expired internal stalk with the fibers stripped away

Figure 60. An expired Milk Weed stalk being
stripped of its outer bark and silky inner fibers.

and the outer skin still clinging to the silky inner bark. If
the fibers were to have been used for a hunting bow string,
or for any fancy work, the outer skin would have been
removed, either by first soaking, then washing away, or
by rubbing the entire mass between the hands so that the
outer skin crumbles away.

Nettle *(Urtica spp.)*, Bull Nettle, Stinging Nettle

Nettle, a.k.a. Bull Nettle, or Stinging Nettle, is another
of those plants that were used primarily for fiber and only
peripherally as a weaving element. Most folks who've done
any appreciable hiking in the western US or Canada have
blundered into a stand of Stinging Nettle at least once,
but never twice. Brushing into a patch of Nettle might
be compared with someone holding your hand in a bees'
nest, then over a batch of burning coals as a remedy to
the stings. When fully mature, nettle plants may be four
to eight feet tall with a coating of fuzz that you may not
notice, *at first*. Once a person has the pleasure of first hand
contact with this fuzz, there is little question as to why it's
called Stinging Nettle.

Figure 61. Bull (Stinging) Nettle along a highway in Gorman, off I-5 north of Los Angeles. Note expired stalks in middle right.

For basketry or cordage purposes, fibers are processed much as are those of Milk Weed; i.e., the very thin, outer, brownish gray skin is rubbed or washed off and the inner bark, which is tannish brown, is stripped away from the pulpy interior. The tan expired stalks, as shown in the far right-center of Figure 61, are gathered after the parent plant has gone dormant for the season and the corpse is fully dead but not putrefied. They are still usable after the new stalks start growing in the spring (again, see Figure 61). The fibers are processed by first cutting away the tiny branches, using relatively new leather gloves. The main stalks are then placed on a flat wood surface and pounded with a flat piece of wood or soft (?) hammer. This breaks the interior pulpy core into small, one inch (+/-) long fragments, leaving the fibrous inner bark more-or-less intact. The fragmented interior is next peeled away from the inner bark (fibers), and the resulting fibers are tied into coils or *hanks* for later use.

Figure 62. An expired Nettle stalk
which has been pounded to release its fibers.

When fully processed and washed, Nettle fibers have a rather dull sheen, and are a silky whitish tan in color, but not quite as white as Milk Weed nor as red as Indian Hemp. They are stronger than Yucca fibers but less than Milk Weed or Indian Hemp. Use of the fibers is pretty much the same as for Yucca, Milk Weed, Agave, or Indian Hemp.

Most western US basket makers, except for southern California people, rarely used fibers for coiled or twined basketry. On rare occasions, a collector may happen onto a Modoc twined basket with a coiled-type "start" composed of Nettle fibers. Brian Bibby (personal contact) states that such "starts" are not uncommon on Modoc baskets, but I have seen only two in my entire life, one of which I "own" (provide residence for). Both observations were made on the same day several moons ago. Figure 63 shows the "start" from that basket.

Parenthetically, some of the western American Indian tribes use fresh Nettle greens much like Popeye used spinach. Apparently, the irritating fuzz does not appear when the leaves first emerge and that fuzz is dissolved when cooked. Use of Nettle as a pot-herb is kind of like using

Poison Oak leaves as an eye wash, which was actually the case by early southern California Indians...**don't you go there!** I have, but I'm Indian!

One of the other fibers used extensively by early American

Figure 63. Nettle fiber in the "start" of a twined Modoc basket.

Indians was Indian Hemp (Dog Bane, or *Apocynum spp.*). Indian Hemp is probably the most user friendly and unquestionably the strongest of the native fibers. It is also the most widespread of the fiber plants. There is, however, minimal reported use of this fiber in North American basketry, so it will not be treated in any detail herein.

Palm *(Washingtonia filifera)*

Most people today associate palm trees with coconuts, beaches, and girls in skimpy grass skirts swaying to the strum of a ukulele. Not so in southern California, where Indians associate palms trees with sexy young Indian girls in skimpy shredded bark skirts making baskets as they sway to the beat of a chorus of deer hoof rattles! (I think). The Palm trees used for basketry are located in the romantic Palm Springs area and don't yield coconuts.

Washingtonia palms are native to a few wet canyons,

or equally fewer and wetter oases in an otherwise hot, arid
Colorado Desert, like Palm Springs (as shown in Figure 64)
or Twentynine Palms, or the Imperial Valley in southern
California. Many are at or below sea level, although almost
always in oases or in steep canyons where water is at or near
the surface, which in itself is kind of rare. The commercial
date palm trees growing in the Coachella Valley near Indio
or Valerie Jean are only vaguely related to the indigenous
Washingtonia filifera palm. This native tree is related to the
"fan palms", which means the fronds are nearly round, or
oval, and radiate out like a fan used in Shakespeare's days
(I think; I wasn't paying much attention to fans in those
days). The fronds' stems are about four feet long and lined
with teeth similar to a White Shark's jaws, only worse.

Inasmuch as most desert Indian basket makers, living

*Figure 64. A cluster of Washingtonia Palms in
Palm Canyon (Cahuilla Indian Reservation) near
Palm Springs, southern California.*

almost at or below sea level, were limited as to available
basketry plants, palm leaves (fronds) served very well
because one frond would supply almost a moon's worth

of weaving, and were easily split to a usable width, and several feet long. Although Palm leaf material was (is) readily available and easy to prepare, it is of a lesser quality than is Sumac or Juncus, which it was used as a substitute for.

When Palm leaf is found in a basket, the chances are 199-to-1 that the basket was created by a Desert Cahuilla weaver from, or near, Palm Springs, in Riverside County, California.

To recognize Palm Leaf in a basket, break out your trusty $4.98 (plus tax) magnifier and look for (1) a dusty light brown or dark tan color, (2) perhaps six to eight deep striations per stitch, (3) one or several mid-ribs down the center of most stitches, (4) a well-worn general appearance, and (5) a texture not unlike dirty, oily, well worn, crepe paper, only more so, as seen in Figure 65.

Although Palm Leaf was reasonably easy to obtain, and

Figure 65. Palm Leaf as a stitching material in a Desert Cahuilla basket from the author's collection. The dark material is dyed Juncus. Note the Bound Under Fag End Stitch (BUFES) in lower left, and "clipped fag end" center foreground.

even easier to split into usable weaver strands, it was used only when other materials were not available, or, when the basket was created for sale to a tourist. In the latter case, wearability was not a concern, and besides ... once the basket was sold, there was no money back guarantee.

Rabbit Bush (*Chrysothamnus nauseosus ssp.*)

Hopi basket weavers of Central Arizona are some of the few western US Indian basket makers that use wicker as a weaving style. Shoots from the Rabbit Bush seem to be their favorite plant material, although Yucca leaves and even Arizona Bear Grass was also used, for non-wicker work. Rabbit Bush is a low growing shrub (up to four feet tall) with almost perpetual yellow blossoms, as shown in Figure 66.

Rabbit Bush can be found almost anywhere west of

Figure 66. Rabbit Bush along the I-5 Fwy. near Gorman, California. Note plants in the background. Photo was taken in late October, well past blooming season for most plants.

the Atlantic Ocean, east of the Pacific Ocean, and south of the North Pole. However, it seems to prefer desert, or even high desert climates, such as in much of New Mexico,

Arizona, California, and the Plateau region, where rainfall is not excessive. Shoots are quite small in diameter and, when proposed as a basketry material by the Hopis, are frequently dyed vivid colors which easily fade if exposed to any appreciable amount of sunlight. Under a $4.98 (plus tax) magnifier, Rabbit Bush can be recognized by its thin bark which, when fresh, is greenish gray but shrivels and cracks with age, much like mud puddles in Death Valley. If your magnifier is really good, say 7x to 10x, you will find tiny bits of fuzz, which suggests that there is a year's supply of dust clinging to the shoot, which is not really the case. If the shoot was peeled and trimmed for size, as it usually is, the surface may show longitudinal scratches, or grooves, as can be seen in Figure 67.

Note that the sticks in the above photo are very deeply

Figure 67. Rabbit Bush in a Hopi cradle. Note what appears to be a very fine fuzz, particularly in those shoots in the upper right.

grooved and appear almost as though they are ribbed. These grooves are probably due to shrinkage. In most cases, Rabbit Bush is used whole, not split.

In some older Hopi cradles, Rabbit Bush was the only plant material available and was used undyed. When such a cradle is found, it is usually quite old, or at least in the "old style." This is not always true, in that the author has a very nice miniature Hopi cradle in his collection that was constructed in this "old style" but was created within the last decade and was purchased at the Heard Museum in Phoenix, Arizona.

Red Bud (*Ceris occidentalis*)

If one were to lay every known western American Indian basket and cradle end-to-end, they would reach (like that famous old sourdough said) from thar to thar! Having said that, it is safe to say that Red Bud would probably be represented as often as any other one plant material, except perhaps for Willow.

Inasmuch as this author has never been from thar to thar, the above statement is pure conjecture. However, one should never doubt that Red Bud is one of the more popular basketry materials in the western US. The plant itself can be found as far south as the "Back Country" of San Diego County, in southern California, and as far north as a fast car can travel in ten sleeps. One sleep is a sage old Indian saying which describes how far a person can travel from a motel, one morning, to another motel that evening.

In most environs, a Red Bud plant is a tall shrub or short tree that may reach ten to fifteen feet in height, as shown in Figure 68. This specific tree is in the author's favorite deer hunting country of Yolo County, approximately forty miles northwest of Sacramento, California, and is periodically "pruned" by the author, as well as the deer, so as to secure long, first year shoots next year. Like many shrubs, the more severe the pruning, the better is the first year growth the following year. In some areas basket weavers, and highway maintenance crews, prune the plant down to the bare nubbins which forces new shoots almost as long as King Kong's arm (I think).

Figure 68. A Red Bud tree in Yolo County, central California.

Figure 69. Leaves on a Red Bud tree in early spring.
Note accumulation of dew on the leaves.

The leaves, pictured in Figure 69, are primarily for recognition purposes. Note that they are heart shaped with a noticeable fold down the center. In the evening the leaf folds up when it goes to sleep, and then unfolds when it wakes up the next morning. In the autumn, they turn a pleasant yellow before being shed.

In the summer months Red Bud trees (shrubs) bear numerous seed pods not unlike sweet peas, only on a tree. Sometimes there may be a dozen pods borne in one cluster, each pod being upwards of four inches long. The pods mature in early-mid summer but cling to the tree, often until the following spring.

Red Bud shoots are gathered in the late autumn, or winter, when the bark turns a brick-red. Some basket makers contend that Red Bud shoots should not be used until they have cured for almost a year. They further contend that aging deepens the brick-red bark and makes for a better pattern material.

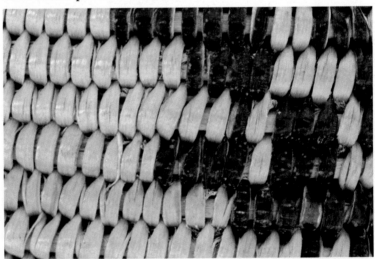

Figure 70. Red Bud as a pattern material on a field of Big Leaf Maple in a Maidu basket from the author's collection.

Red Bud is easily recognized once it enters a basket by that deep red bark and the many tiny white specks on the bark. Indeed, the presence of these tiny specks, which botanists call lenticels, are a dead give-away to Red Bud in a basket. There are several other materials that approximate the same color, and several contain tiny lenticels. However, Red Bud is perhaps the only material that contains both the lenticels and the deep brick-red color.

Figure 71. Whole, peeled Red Bud sticks (warps), and unpeeled Red Bud wefts, in a Sierra Mono Cradle by Leona Chepo.

Figure 71 illustrates the use of whole peeled Red Bud shoots as warps (long vertical sticks) plus split unpeeled Red Bud wefts (diagonally twined horizontal elements) in a Sierra Mono receiving cradle (for a new-born baby). This cradle was created in 2001 by Leona Chepo, a well known Sierra Mono basket weaver of North Fork, northeast of Fresno, California. Inasmuch as many Sierra Mono weavers use both peeled Red Bud and Chaparral in their cradles, it is often difficult telling the two apart. The two are very similar and often are indistinguishable.

The reader is referred to Figure 22 regarding Chaparral as sticks in a similar cradle created by Michelle Smith. Note the bud scars in Michelle Smith's cradle, with the "upside down two eyes and a mouth" where the bud scar is, which is quite different from the sticks in Figure 71.

Occasionally a basketry nut will find a basket containing Red Bud that has a surface coating of what appears to be a silvery mildew "Bloom." On first blush the coating appears very similar to a mold or mildew. However, when viewed through a $4.98 (plus tax) magnifier, the coating closely resembles frost which accumulates on your Ice Cream container in the freezer. The bloom crystals actually stand upright on the Red Bud bark, but can be seen only with the aid of a good magnifier. Some unwitting museum officials throw up their hands and rush frantically to cleanse the ailing basket. Most "old timers", like the author, would willingly kill just for the privilege of holding such a basket for one precious moment. This bloom is a crystallization of certain chemicals in Red Bud bark and is therefore a positive clue as to the antiquity of the basket, which doesn't start this crystallization process for many many moons (plus a few eclipses).

Sedge root (*Carex spp.*), "White Root"

Both Jepson and Moerman list dozens of Sedge species (Jepson lists twenty-eight while Moerman lists twenty-two). All are moisture-loving plants which may be found in almost every climatic environment in the western US, Canada, and Alaska, except perhaps on the Mendenhall Glacier. Some species are tall and rank, while others are low-growing with a long horizontal rhizome/root. The roots of some species are used in basketry throughout much of central California, as well as the Sierra foothills, the southern Cascades, and parts of California's Northwest. This root is used mostly in coiled ware, but also to a lesser degree in twining. Sedge root is also used occasionally in the Pacific Northwest, but not to the extent that the Yokuts or Pomos use(d) it.

Sedge roots are harvested, usually in the late autumn, by prying up the rhizome with a digging stick (never a shovel, which tends to severe the rhizome). In many areas, basket makers cultivate the soil and remove rocks, weeds, and deleterious materials. "Deleterious" is a sage old Indian word which translates into American as undesirable).

The rhizome itself has an outer fleshy coating, which is

stripped away leaving an inner woody core, which, in turn, is split into two longitudinal strands. Even after removing the outer coating the woody inner layer must be scraped or rubbed clean of its chalky surface which is hard to remove entirely, and thus clings to the inner core. This chalky coating gives Sedge root its distinctive texture.

To recognize Sedge in the field the novice should remember the sage old Indian saying "Sedges have edges." Translated into American, that means the above-ground stems are triangular in cross section rather than round. Most Sedge plants, used for basketry, are found near streams or in damp areas where the soil is sandy or silty, as shown in Figure 72. Note that a solitary plant somewhat resembles a solitary Bear Grass plant from northern California.

Figure 72. Sedge growing along a stream bed in Riverside County, southern California. Note an invasion of wild grape vines, with large roundish leaves and vines which are taking over.

When looking for Sedge root in a basket, the first thing you should notice is that although weaver strands are light tan in color, their surfaces are slightly powdered, or chalky, and vary in hue from an ivory-white-tan to a rich honey-oily-tan. As might be expected, variation in color and texture seems to be attributable to the geographical area. This variegated color and texture gives the finished basket a somewhat "laundered" appearance, which is so characteristic of Sedge root.

Figure 73. Dr. Julia Parker holding a basket of Sedge root.

*Figure 74. Sedge root and
Red Bud in the above Julia Parker basket.*

Figure 75. A coiled basketry "start"
using Sedge from the San Joaquin Valley floor.
Note its lighter color as compared with Figure 74.

When viewed through your trusty $4.98 (plus tax) magnifier, the weaver strand is half-round, unlike many weaving materials which are flattish. Figure 73 is a photo of Dr. Julia Parker creating a Sedge root mini burden basket which now resides in the author's collection.

When found in a basket, it is quite easy to distinguish Sedge root from, say, Willow or Peeled Red Bud, because Sedge root, when viewed from a slight distance, has a mottled, slightly chalky color/texture, which ranges from almost chalky white to light tan, whereas peeled Red Bud, or Sumac, or Willow have relatively smooth, homogeneous surfaces.

The Sedge roots used in Dr. Parker's basket were obtained in the higher foothills of the Sierra Nevada Mountain range and tend to be much darker in color than Sedge gathered from lower elevations. As the basket ages, the chalky texture of Sedge root materials tend to wear thin and in a very old basket, Sedge root may somewhat resemble aged Willow or even Big Leaf Maple.

Spruce root *(Picea sitchensis)*, Sitka Spruce root

In much of the Pacific Northwest, specifically Washington, Canada, and southern Alaska, Cedar and Spruce are the most commonly used Indian basketry plants. Cedar is used either as a shoot or root, and Spruce is primarily from the root. Sitka Spruce seems to be the most commonly used species of Spruce, which is found along the Pacific Northwest coast from Klamath, California, north into Alaska, virtually at the sea shore, where it thrives on coastal fog. Figure 76 pictures a lone Spruce tree near Klamath, California.

*Figure 76. A Sitka Spruce tree
near Klamath in northern California.*

Although Spruce root is used in the coastal northwest portions of California, its use really blossoms out when it reaches the British Columbia coast, where it, along with Red Cedar, is the dominant basketry material of the Haida and Tlingit people.

To obtain a weaving strand (per Lena Horn), the first step is to select a young Sitka Spruce tree growing in sandy soil, generally near the beach. A trunk diameter of six inches to slightly over one foot is preferred for smaller roots, whereas larger trees generally yield larger roots. A trench is dug about six inches into the soil fairly close to the trunk until a root is located. That root may be as small as the lead in a lead pencil or as large as a broom stick. The root is then uncovered for a distance that ranges from several feet to as long as your Chrysler mini van.

After harvesting, a root is either peeled of its bark, *in situ* (*in situ* is a sage old Indian word meaning ... in the field were you found it) or it is coiled and taken home to be de-barked before the root dries out. To prepare the root, which is reasonably dark reddish brown, a fire is started in the sandy soil and allowed to burn down to red hot coals. The coiled root is then held over the coals until the sap begins to sizzle and the bark bubbles up, after which it is stripped away revealing an ivory-white woody core. The root is next split into halves revealing a rather glossy surface (the cambium layer) and a fibrous-woody inner core. If the root is fairly large, the root is split into one-quarters or one-eighths. The number of splittings depends upon how great is the root diameter.

Next the outer surface is separated from the inner core, much as the core of Sumac or Willow is separated from the cambium layer. In this process the glossy outer surface, just under the outer bark, (the cambium layer) is saved for a weft in finer baskets. The inner material, referred to herein as the core, may be saved as a fibrous-woody weft for cradle boards or large utility baskets.

Where a large utility basket is proposed, a considerable amount of internal material is needed, thus a large root is harvested, which yields a great amount of inner core. If the basket is to be very small, only small roots are harvested and the inner core is discarded.

In a basket, Spruce root tends to have a deep tan-almost-brown hue, and, with the naked eye, be slightly glossy. Under a $4.98 (plus tax) magnifier the material appears to be slightly fibrous with traces of a lustrous sheen. Figure 77 shows Spruce root which was used to wrap the frame of a Yurok Cradle from Crescent City, northern California.

Figure 77. Spruce root on the frame of a Yurok cradle by Loren Bommelyn from Crescent City, California.

Spruce root is generally several shades darker than is most other Pacific Northwest wrapping materials, such as Hazel or Grape root but not as dark, or red, as Cedar root. Under a magnifier, it also appears quite fibrous. If the cambium layer is being inspected, it may be almost as glossy as Cedar bark. The primary difference between Cedar and Spruce is that Cedar bark has numerous but tiny longitudinal striations with a gloss, whereas Spruce root is slightly less glossy and slightly more cottony. Inasmuch as Sitka Spruce, which is the main source of Spruce root, grows only along the Pacific coast, which is subject to frequent fog, and only north of about Klamath, California, it is not used to any extent by inland basket makers.

Sumac (*Rhus trilobata*), "Sour Berry", "Basket Weed"

Sumac is reported to grow almost everywhere except on the planet Mars and on the South Pole, and was used primarily in coiled basketry throughout the Far West and southwestern USA. In California it was rarely used in twining, except occasionally as vertical warps in utility baskets. That is not to say that it wasn't used by some

Sierra Nevada folks in their cradles. It is (was), however, used very extensively by the Nevada, Arizona, and New Mexico weavers for both coiling and twining because 1) it is readily available, 2) it is so easy to split, trim and size, 3) it is so strong and durable, 4) it takes on a beautiful patina with age, 5) it is user-friendly, and 6) like a pretty maiden, it is so white when young and innocent!

Sumac is a half-brother to Poison Oak and if you, the reader, are not intimately familiar with both, then you are strongly encouraged to not try harvesting Sumac. The author has been gathering and processing Sumac for many many (hundreds of) moons, and he thought that he knew right from wrong ... wrong! Several years ago he was splitting a bunch of Sumac shoots only to discover that some of the shoots he was splitting were Poison Oak. Don't you do a dumb thing like that. The author can do it because he's Indian, and you know what they say about Indians and poison oak!

Sumac is a low growing, vine-like shrub that rarely exceeds three to four feet in height. Figure 78 depicts a somewhat typical patch of Sumac. First year shoots may

Figure 78. A patch of Sumac, plus Poison Oak, rattlesnakes, rocks, etc. on Salt Creek in Yolo County, California.

reach three to five feet in length and about the diameter of a skinny lead pencil. Second year growth is normally not used because of twigs and branches which distract from the usability of a shoot. If you are really fortunate and a fire burned over your Sumac patch, you may find the new shoots starting to grow almost before the flames died down, and, depending upon the timing of the fire, this new growth may, in a few months, well exceed a normal year's growth. Now don't you go starting a fire just to improve the Sumac crop! Smokey, that little bear with a play-like ranger's hat, frowns on such fires.

Sumac shoots can be gathered almost anytime they are long enough; i.e., several feet or more. First year growth is quite easy to recognize because the bark is reddish brown with rarely any branching or even any buds or leaves. There may also be tiny gray splotches somewhat like those on Red Bud if the shoot has fully matured. After the first year, the bark turns from reddish brown to a dark gray and buds or branches start to form, which lessens the quality of the weaver strand. Incidentally, if a bud or twig is encountered, there will be a tiny knot, or flaw, in the weaver strand, which, in southern California, is often referred to as a "dimple." Dimples are okay on a lady but not on her basket.

When gathering Sumac, you will almost always be confronted with a patch similar to that in Figure 78. Such patches make great homes for squirrels, rabbits, mice, and rattlesnakes. Before even thinking about going into such a patch, there is certain etiquette you must follow. First, spiritually (mentally) say hello to Mr. Rattlesnake. You need not verbalize but you should communicate spiritually with him. Tell him you plan him no harm and the chances are 99 to 1 you won't even see him. Several years ago I was gathering Sumac at the very patch shown in Figure 78. I followed my own advice and spoke to Mr. Rattlesnake before entering the patch. Sure enough, there he was, not three feet away. I looked at him, smiled, and said "Hello my friend." He looked back and kind-of smiled in return. I commented on what a nice home he had and asked permission to visit. I also told him that I planned no harm to him, his wife, nor his kids. At this he visibly relaxed. Never once did he coil up, rattle, or strike a combative pose. We spoke about his home and how nice it was. I inquired into the health of his wife and kids, and he reacted favorably. To show my confidence and friendliness, I told him I wanted a Sumac shoot about eighteen inches from his head. I then *carefully and slowly* reached down with my pocket knife and harvested that shoot. Never once did he take an offensive action. I then thanked him for his hospitality and left. The moral of this story is ... *If you are entering a snake's living room, remember, it is his house, not yours, and he has the right to invite you in, or to keep you out.*

Figure 79 is a photo of Sumac after the leaves have turned red in the autumn. Note that the leaves are almost the same as those on Poison Oak. Although not readily apparent in that photo, there are several first year shoots which have the distinctive reddish-brown bark, as contrasted with the gray of second year growth. One is in the lower center, standing almost vertically to about the center of the photo. The second is in the lower left and slanted up-left at about thirty degrees.

Figure 79. Sumac leaves turning red in the autumn. Note the similarity to Poison Oak leaves, and the reddish brown first year shoot in the lower center standing almost vertical, and another in the lower left, leaning slightly to the left.

When working with Sumac the first thing you notice is the resinous feel of the peeled or split strand, as well as its strong taste/odor. If you think that you are working with Sumac and you do not feel the resin or smell the distinctive odor, beware! Poison Oak looks almost identical, but doesn't smell or have the resin.

When looking for Sumac in a basket, press into service your trusty $4.98 (plus tax) magnifier, and note that the surface of a Sumac stitch is reasonably smooth but contains a very faint stripe of a resinous material deeply engrained under the slightly translucent surface. It is this resinous streak that differentiates Sumac from Willow or Hazel. The photo in Figure 80 is of Sumac in a "Mission" basket. This specific basket was made in 1921 by a Mrs. Neva Chapulli, a Cupeno lady from the San Ysidro region (Los Coyotes Reservation) near Warners Hot Springs, in northeastern San Diego County, southern California. Please note the very pronounced BUFES (Bound Under Fag End Stitch) a.k.a. "Mission Stitch," so characteristic of a southern California "Mission" basket. This stitch is actually a half-hitch thrown in the fag, or beginning, end of a new weaver strand.

Figure 80. Sumac as a stitching material in a 1921 basket by Mrs. Nevas Chapulli, a San Diego County Cupeno lady.

It has been said (by the author) that Sumac improves with age. Although it begins life almost stark white, it soon darkens to a rich honey-tan and forms a patina. It is this patina that sets many "Mission" baskets apart from other coiled ware. Many museums and private collectors do not like a person to touch a basket with their grubby hands. However, your author, feels that handling a basket (with clean hands) tends to keep it from getting rigor mortis, and may (?) help in developing a patina.

Tules (*Scirpus spp.*), Bulrush

The reader will remember that Tules were discussed in at least a modicum of detail on several previous pages. Only there we called it Bulrush. That is because we were discussing the root, not the stalk. The plant is known by both names; i.e., Tules (which is kind of a categorical word), and Bulrush (which is also categorical but more folksy).

The above ground portion of the plant is (was) used almost nationwide for everything from creating a basket to adorning your wife's evening gown (if she was a pre-contact American Indian debutant). Today we see examples of Tules being used by early Indians (and even some non-Indians) in making canoes, baskets, cradles, houses, mats, duck decoys, dolls, braided doodads (gee gaws,) plus a myriad of other "stuff." In fact, the term "Tules" has even been used to connotate a far-out place which is cold, damp and ... you shouldn't go there!

In the subject case, the term "Tules" is confined to that plant which is used in creating basketry in western North America. When found growing along the edge of a waterway, the uninformed, with only one good eye open, may mistake Tules for giant Juncus, which it isn't! Juncus is a member of the Reed family while Tule is part of the Sedge (*Cyperacae*) family. Now ... do you know any more than you did 1/2 minute ago?

Most Tules are found near or actually in standing water, where they can take a bath now and then, as shown in Figure 81. Perhaps the reason Tules and Juncus are often

Figure 81. Tules growing on the edge of a lake in Santa Barbara.

confused is the fact that both have similar inflorescence and

Figure 82 Inflorescence and stalks of Tules. Note the round leafless stalks as contrasted with Cattails.

both have a round, reed-like upper portion. Inflorescence is an old Indian term which most basket weavers call seed heads.

Stems of a growing plant are a deep forest-green color, they stand at least five feet tall, and are slightly triangular in cross section near their bottom (earth end). After maturing, the stems turn a dirty, brownish tan color and often show mildew splotches. Prior to being used in basketry, the green must be bleached out, usually by leaving them in the direct sun. Like large Juncus reeds, they have no leaves, and their stalks are pithy or slightly hollow.

Basketry weaver strands are created by splitting the stalk into long thin strands and using only the outer, fairly smooth surface as shown in Figure 83. In a few cases, the split strands are twisted to form a sort-of cord that is used by the Modoc and some other weavers as a weaver strand.

Tules are (were) used widely in basketry of northeastern

Figure 83. Dyed and undyed Tule used in a Modoc hat.

California, southeastern Oregon, then almost to the north pole, where weavers had to stop before falling over the edge (although falling over the edge has not been verified, recently). When viewed in a basket, Tules may tend to have a slight glaze somewhat resembling old, dirty Bear Grass, except Tule has much deeper and more pronounced longitudinal striations, whereas Bear Grass has a more glossy sheen and an almost oily striated texture.

Chumash cradles were created almost exclusively using Tule stalks over a "Y" shaped Willow frame as shown in Figure 84.

Rosemary (Castillo) Lopez, Jose Castillo, and Anna

Figure 84. A Chumash mini cradle, by Anna Campbell, made of Tule, cotton. and a forked Willow limb.

Campbell currently make Chumash basketry cradles using large Tule stalks, albeit few, if any, Chumash babies are still carried in a basketry cradle. A miniature Chumash cradle created by Anna Campbell for the author is shown in Figure 84.

Willow (*Salix spp.*) shoots

It has been said in previous chapters that such-and-such a plant is probably the most commonly used plant for basketry anywhere in western North America. Well, the same can be said about Willow. The difference is that Willow is (was) used for almost every conceivable purpose

Figure 85. A heavily pruned Willow tree in Craig Park, Fullerton, California, showing the resulting long whippy limbs ideally suited to creating weaver strands for coiled ware.

around the tipi; e.g., tipi rafters, tipi shingles, tipi siding, tipi chairs, tipi tables; and then to add a few more, baskets, granaries, bows, arrows, baby cradles, women's skirts, cordage, mats, etc., etc., etc. In fact, if Mrs. Ima Indian got a headache, she cured it with a Willow bark tea, the original source of aspirin. It didn't seem to matter to most Indians which species of Willow was used, as long as it was easy to obtain, which it usually is.

Ironically, even though most North American Indians used Willow in their basketry, those native people in southern California did not use it in their coiled baskets, perhaps because Sumac serves the same purpose and is much easier to gather and prepare. Sumac is also much more durable than is Willow. Notwithstanding the above, southern California Indians did use Willow boughs in manufacturing their acorn granaries (storage vessels), but avoided Willow in their baskets almost like some guys avoid paying alimony.

Moerman describes forty-one species or varieties of Willow used by American Indians. The author failed his third grade class in botany, so he normally can't tell one Willow from the next. In his view, if the bark is red, it must be Red Willow. If it grows in an arroyo, then it must be Arroyo Willow. If its leaves are gray, it must be Gray Willow, and if it grows on a sandbar in a river bed, it must be Sand Bar Willow... Right? For our purpose here, and to keep it simple, we will not split hairs and refer to all Willow simply as Willow. That is, unless it is peeled Willow, Willow roots, or Sunburned Willow, (more on Willow root and Sunburned Willow later).

Willow trees or bushes can be found in almost every life zone in the USA. The tree shown in Figures 85 is in Fullerton, southern California. This specific tree was pruned recently, which explains the long whippy limbs. Each species, or variety, of Willow reacts slightly differently as it is processed into a basket. Because the author does not claim to be a botanist, differentiating between the various Willow varieties in a basket is beyond his scope of knowledge.

Figure 86 shows Willow as a weft in a Paiute hat. Note

the leaf scars, which in most cases are nearly round and somewhat resemble a pin prick. The specific type of twining used in this hat is a classic case of plain diagonal twining.

Willow in a basket, either as a warp, a weft, or a weaver

Figure 86. A detail of Willow wefts in a Paiute hat from the author's collection. Note the numerous leaf scars and irregular widths. Note also the classic use of diagonal twining.

strand, has a reasonably smooth surface with only minute striations. When fresh, weaver strands tend to be almost white with a slight cottony texture, which tends to darken to a soft honey-tan or sand color in only a few moons, particularly if the basket is left exposed to sunlight or incandescent lighting.

Occasionally Willow weaver strands, or wefts, will show a leaf scar where a leaf or twig wanted to get started. These scars somewhat resemble a shallow round hole, which is in contrast to the Hazel Kink, or the leaf scar from other weaver strands. Although there are slight differences in leaf scars in different species, the reader should beware of drawing cast-in-concrete conclusions based upon what a leaf scar looks like, except perhaps a Hazel Kink, as shown in Figure 87.

Figure 87. A Hazel Kink in the middle warp and in the lower center weft.

Sunburned Willow (*Salix spp.*)

The Paiute people, east of the Sierra Nevada Mountains, are somewhat unique in their use of inner Willow bark to create a brown pattern material. Many Willow shoots have

Figure 88. Sunburned Willow in a Paiute basket from the author's collection.

a dark gray-green outer bark, plus a pale greenish white

inner bark, the latter of which is referred to by botanists as *Phloem*. If subjected to bright sunlight, this *phloem* turns a pale rusty brown color vaguely similar to Alder dyed material and is often referred to as Sunburned Willow, or Winter Willow, as seen in Figure 88. Under a magnifier, it appears rather rough textured, almost like the interior of a root, as contrasted to the smooth surface of normal Willow.

Sunburned Willow is relatively common in that portion of northern Paiute country north of Owen's Lake and south of Mono Lake in eastern California and western Nevada.

Willow root *(Salix spp.)*

A previous chapter addressed Willow, in general, and made passing reference to Willow root. In this chapter, Willow root is discussed. In Figure 89, Mrs. Verna Reece is shown harvesting a Willow root near her home in Happy Camp, Siskiyou County, California.

As might be expected, there is a sandy bar along the edge

Figure 89. Mrs. Verna Reece digging Willow roots on the banks of the Klamath River near Happy Camp, California.

of many northern California rivers, from which Sand Bar
Willows grow quite profusely. Where beaches are primarily
sandy silt, roots are quite easy to dig. Figure 90 shows the
root Mrs. Reece was harvesting in Figure 89, which is about
the diameter of a thin wooden lead pencil, but four feet
long. (It is pretty hard to see clearly but it loops from one
hand to another and is visible below her sweater.)

Willow roots somewhat resemble commercial cane, as

*Figure 90. Verna Reece holding
the Willow root harvested in Figure 89.*

used in caning chairs, except perhaps a bit more fibrous.
In most cases, roots are round in cross section, very long,
and of a consistent diameter. They are very flexible and can
be wrapped about a very tiny warp without showing any
distress. When viewed very closely, the root may show deep
longitudinal striations, although with a naked eye it may
resemble the smooth cottony surface of other Willow weaver
strands. Many of the baskets from the Klamath River region

of northern California contain a "start", or bottom, of Willow root as a weft, although the warps are generally of Willow shoots. Figure 91 shows Willow root in the bottom of a baby rattle made by Lena Hurd, a Yurok lady, and acquired by the author from Mrs. Hurd in 2007. Quite frequently tiny shreds of inner bark (*phloem*) remain after de-barking, which turn a brownish red color. This material resembles Sunburned Willow, but should not be confused with the latter.

An overall view of Figure 91 suggests that there are

*Figure 91. Willow roots used in the 1.5″
radius base of a Yurok baby rattle by Lena Hurd.*

various twining styles present. The beginning has six warps, of Willow shoots laid in a square pattern, and wrapped by Willow root wefts generally about each two warps. After eight rows of plain diagonal twining, Mrs. Hurd inserted two whorls of red Alder-dyed Woodwardia fern stems. The next whorls contain alternating Bear Grass as false embroidery, and Alder dyed Woodwardia ferns in diagonal twining. This latter style is almost diagnostic of northern California and the Pacific Northwest.

Sand Bar Willow (*Salix spp.*)

There seems to be some minor differences between botanists as to which species of Willow is correctly called Sand Bar, and which species was used by whom, when, and where. Jepson, in his 1925 Manual, refers to Sand Bar Willow as *Salix sessilifolia*, while Moerman, in his 1998 edition, calls it *S. exigua*, but he also says *S. hindsiana* was used extensively in northern and central California as basketry materials. Margaret "Peg" Mathewson, a basketry and plant materials authority from Oregon, told the author that Sand Bar Willow is really Gray Willow. If the botanists can't agree on what Willow should be called by what name, then how can a poor country boy, like Mrs. Farmer's son, be expected to know. For our purposes here we will simply call the plant Sand Bar Willow and let the botanists duke it out.

Figures 92 and 93 show examples of Sand Bar Willow as it grows along the banks of the Klamath River in northern California. Many of the Klamath River weavers (Yurok, Hupa, and Karuk people) gather short, very thin Willow shoots generally in the spring, after sap has begun flowing. During this season the bark is most easily stripped from a fresh shoot, but the fleshy tip of the shoot has not yet started. These shoots are often twelve to eighteen inches long and, when peeled of their bark, are no greater than 1/8 inch in diameter. After being peeled they are sorted for size and used as warps (sticks) in the delicate Karuk, Hupa, and Yurok twined baskets. These sticks are used whole, but because they are so fine and flexible, they make excellent warps, or even wefts, and can be bent and twisted quite easily.

A comment is made in reference to Figure 93, that the shoot shown is too long for most twining uses. To understand this comment the reader must recognize that a warp in most twinned baskets is rarely more than six to ten

Figure 92. Sand Bar Willow along the edge of the Klamath River.

Figure 93. Sand Bar Willow shoots. The longer shoot extending from upper middle to lower right is too long for most twining uses.

inches long, in contrast to that in a coiled basket where the weaver is often three feet long, or longer. In twined baskets a warp shorter than six inches may even be spliced so as to use a much thinner shoot. The predominate thing here is the thinness and flexibility of the warp, and weft.

In the "downstream" regions of the Klamath River, many weavers use thin Hazel sticks in lieu of Willow. Hazel sticks are not as straight as Willow but, according to Verna Reece, are more rigid. Figure 94 illustrates the character and thinness of Willow sticks in a basket created for the author in 2006 by Frank Reece, a Karuk man from Happy Camp in northern California. Frank is the husband of Verna Reece. Both are well respected Karuk weavers. Figure 94 also illustrates use of very thin Sand Bar Willow root as a weft.

When viewed with your $4.98 (plus tax) magnifier, it is

Figure 94. From a Karuk basketry cap by Frank Reece of Happy Camp on the Klamath River, California. The sticks are Willow shoots and the wefts are Willow root.

obvious that Sand Bar Willow sticks do not have the smooth whitish luster that some of the other Willows have.

Woodwardia fern (*Woodwardia spp.*), Giant Chain fern

Both Jepson and Moerman list a number of ferns used to create basketry patterns in northern California and the Pacific Northwest. The species *Woodwardia fimbiata* is perhaps the more commonly used species, but *W. radicans* was (is) also used, depending upon the area under consideration (according to Moerman). Both are similar to a very large, overgrown Bracken fern or a very small Hawaiian tree fern, as shown in Figure 95. Its leaves (fronds) are upwards of four feet long (Jepson says up to eight feet but this may be questionable, he may have been reminiscing on his last trip to Hawaii).

Figure 95. Woodwardia ferns, Siskiyou County, California. Note the amount of undergrowth, dead and decomposing limbs, and leaf mold which fern roots find very warm and fuzzy.

The Woodwardia ferns shown in Figure 95 have fronds approximately four feet in length and are located in the vicinity of the Klamath River approximately ten mile east of the town of Happy Camp, Siskiyou County, California. Other Woodwardia plants are found throughout the Klamath River basin but may not be nearly as long.

Woodwardia ferns are quite common in the more dense forests and in damp areas throughout northern California, and north almost to the north pole. The plants seem to like areas where water is actually at the surface, although they can be found in patches where leaf mold is dense and roots do not have to penetrate hard soil. Like many ferns, they seem to be happiest if they get rained upon about once a week, at least in the dry season. If it doesn't rain, then a little water over their feet sure makes them happy. The ferns in Figure 95 are thriving in a deep forest of Pines, Fir, Cedar, Maple, Dogwood, Bramble, Black Berries, Poison Oak, and even a patch of Juncus. This author has seen Woodwardia Ferns growing vigorously in logging road cut banks where water is seeping from the hillside. He has also seen Woodwardia in rock crevices within a few hundred yards of the ocean along State Highway 1 in Monterey County, in a botanical garden in Santa Barbara, along an iron-rich stream in San Diego County's mountainous back country near Julian, and even in the author's front yard in urban Orange County. They probably extend well into the Pacific Northwest but I haven't penetrated that far to confirm such a rash statement.

To obtain a weaver strand from Woodwardia ferns, the four foot long (+/-) frond is first stripped of its leaflets leaving a thirty-six to forty-eight inch long "stem" (see Figure 96). This is pounded rather lovingly over a reasonably soft surface, like a granite boulder, until it becomes partially shredded. Two rather thin, yellowish, longitudinal fibers are extracted from each stem, as seen in Figure 96. These are the fibers that are used as basketry plant elements.

In almost all cases, Woodwardia fern weaver strands are dyed a rusty red-brown color using a stain derived from pulverized, or chewed up Alder bark (as discussed in a previous section). This dyed weaver strand is then used as a pattern or overlay material in twined basketry or as ornamentation on cradle boards.

The spots on the leaves in Figure 96 are spores, which are the reproduction organs of a fern. Most Karuk basket makers are careful to leave these in the field when they gather the ferns, so as to assist in propagation.

Figure 96. A Woodwardia leaf stem with leaflets removed. Note the thin yellowish fiber below the main stem. That is the usable portion and is extracted from each side of the stem.

Although the brown color of dyed Woodwardia may appear uniform to the naked eye, under your trusty $4.98 (plus tax) magnifier, it appears rather uneven and fibrous with streaks of darker/lighter color, with a darker streak down the center.

Figure 97 contains a photo of Alder bark dyed Woodwardia fern as it was used in an open ware Hupa basket from the author's collection. In most baskets from northern California, and many from Oregon, Alder dyed Woodwardia fern is accompanied by Bear Grass and Maidenhair fern as either false embroidery or as an overlay.

To a person not intimately acquainted with Alder dyed Woodwardia fern, the material may appear similar to Conifer root; i.e., there are numerous longitudinal striations and it is about the color one would expect in Conifer root. Figure 27 shows Conifer root to be much more fibrous with a relatively coarse texture, sans the rich reddish brown color of Woodwardia fern.

Figure 97. Alder-dyed Woodwardia fern, with a
darker streak down the center of the weft, in a Hupa basket.
The lighter material is Bear Grass.

Yucca fiber (*Yucca whipplei*), Our Lord's Candle

This treatise started out, innocently enough, to be about plant materials use to create western North American Indian baskets; i.e., either as a warp, a weft, a pattern element, a stitching material, or as a foundation. However, the author tends to stray a bit from the game plan. An astute reader, familiar with California or Pacific Northwest baskets, might logically ask "what's Yucca fibers got to do with weaving an Indian basket? They weren't used as a warp, nor as a weft, ...Right?" Yucca leaves and roots were used extensively as stitching materials. However, Yucca fiber is the subject in these paragraphs, which is a common fiber for "starts' in coiled basketry. Figure 98 pictures *Yucca whipplei* plants and expired leaves from which Yucca fibers may be extracted.

To obtain Yucca fibers, your author collects old dead leaves from an expired Yucca plant, such as that pictured in the center-right of Figure 98. The leaves are then pounded with a hammer on a steel anvil until the dried fleshy material is powdered and can be rubbed away. This takes forty-five

*Figure 98. An expired Yucca whipplei (center-right) on
the Angeles Crest Highway north of Los Angeles, California.*

to sixty seconds per leaf and leaves a hank of Yucca fibers
ready for use. The resulting fibers are a dark sand color
and are ideal for use as a "start" in a coiled basket. Figure
99 shows a partially pounded Yucca leaf with the fibers

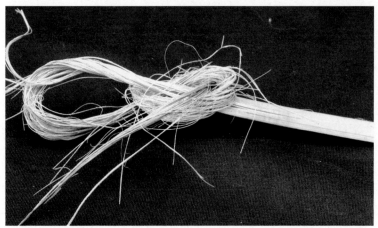

*Figure 99 A Yucca whipplei leaf partially pounded and its Fibers
exposed. The unpounded leaf is on the right.*

exposed on the left. A fairly high percentage of "Mission" baskets weavers used Yucca fiber for their "starts".

If the Yucca fiber was to be used as cordage, or for any other purpose where the color should be stark white, then green living leaves were harvested and pounded until the white fleshy material could be scrubbed clean with water and rubbing. This is about ten times slower than the hammer/anvil method.

Yucca leaf (*Yucca elata*), Spanish Bayonet, Soaptree.

Yucca elata leaves are used extensively as stitching material in coiled ware and as plaiting elements by 1) the Tohono O'odham (formerly Papago), 2) some early Akimel O'otham (formerly Pima), 3) the Hopi (still are Hopi), and 4) some of the Apaches (who were Apaches until we sicked the US Army on them). Figure 100 shows a group of *Yucca elata* plants on the Tohono O'odham Rez west of Tucson, Arizona. Unlike *Yucca whipplei*, whose leaves do not die until the plant blossoms, many times, then dies. As seen in Figure 100, leaves of these plants simply mature and die back but the plant continues to grow.

Figure 100. Yucca elata plants, Tohono O'odham Reservation, Arizona. See Figure 101 for details of these coarse leaves.

Figure 101. A closer view of
Yucca elata showing the coarse leaves.

A study of pre-contact basketry suggests that Yucca leaves were used extensively throughout most of the southwestern US, not only for basketry, but also for mats, utility items, sandals, and whatever else Mrs. Ima Indian, or Mr. Alsoa Indian needed.

Inasmuch as the Tohono O'odham people are reputed to have created more baskets than all the rest of the Indians of the Southwest, combined, and because they are the primary users of Yucca leaves in their basketry, most of the narrative herein is oriented toward these people. Their coiled ware contains green, tan, or white Yucca leaves (mostly *Y. elata*) wrapped about a foundation of split Bear Grass leaves. Although Yucca leaves are normally a deep green when mature, the leaves gathered by many Tohono O'odham weavers are those from the inner core; i.e., those leaves not yet mature and still almost white in color.

The numerous longitudinal striations and the rather crepe paper appearance of *Yucca elata* are quite noticeable in Figure 102. Also, a close look at the stub ends of weaver

Figure 102. **Yucca elata** *(white),* **Yucca root** *(red),
and Devil's Claw (black) in a Tohono O'odham basket, a
gift of Bob Hickman, Old Sacramento.*

strands in the middle right and upper center of Figure 102
shows what was referred to earlier as a clipped end in a
coiled basket. The clipped end reveals a rather cellular
interior of the Yucca wrapping material because this
wrapping material was taken from the outside surface of
the Yucca leaf but also contains some of the cellular inner
core. The brownish red pattern material is Banana Yucca
root, as discussed in the following paragraphs.

Yucca root *(Yucca bacata, brevifolia,* and *mohavensis)*

Yucca root was used quite extensively throughout the
southwestern US. Among the Serranos of San Bernardino
County and some northern Paiutes, *Yucca brevifolia*
(Joshua Tree) was the predominate species, albeit Mohave
Yucca was often used. In fact, there are few people who can
differentiate between the two, once into a basket. Almost
all of the Yuccas have a root ranging from reddish-brown,
to deep maroon, to pale orange, or even yellow. In Arizona,
Yucca bacata provides a deep, rich, almost carmine red
surface that is used extensively by the Tohono O'odham,

sometimes by the Akimel O'otham, and some of the New Mexico Apaches. Figure 103 pictures a *Yucca bacata* plant near Sunset Overlook on Highway 17 in northern Arizona.

The plant in Figure 103 is about four feet tall, with long

Figure 103. **Yucca bacata** *near Sunset Overlook on the Route 17 freeway north of Phoenix, Arizona.*

thick, whippy leaves and is somewhat unkempt. Joshua Tree (*Yucca brevifolia*) has similar roots, but the plant is dramatically different; i.e., although Joshua Tree is a Yucca, it grows like a tree. It may stand twenty or thirty feet tall, and its leaves are much shorter (hence the name *brevifolia*), and much more orderly. Figure 104 shows moderate size Joshua Trees near the I-15 freeway west of Victorville in southern California.

When found in a basket, Yucca root really jumps out at you. Unlike many pattern materials, the root is usually split in half, rather than thirds, so the surface appears half-round rather than flat, and is normally smooth with few striations. This half-round form is also present in Joshua Tree and Mohave Yucca roots. The colors are not dramatically

CHAPTER 5

IDENTIFICATION CLUES

If the reader has really digested the preceding discussions regarding plant characteristics, it is not all that difficult to identify most plants after they are incorporated into a basket. However, if the basket has been mistreated, or is very old, identifying a specific material may not be as obvious as you are lead, herein, to believe. Not to worry! There are often clues that give the thing away. This chapter addresses only one of many such clues; clues which are often subtle or even negative, but they are clues, none-the-less, and often quite elementary (*my dear Watson*). Only one example is given here, and that is merely to show the thought processes a person often must go through to identify a given plant material.

In this chapter, for instance, we are interested in determining exactly what peeled Red Bud looks like after it has lived in a basket for almost a century and has lost many of its easily recognized characteristics. Peeled Red Bud is never real easy to identify, particularly if the basket is dirty, soiled, faded, or otherwise mistreated. The narrative which follows deals not so much with details, but more with the overall process which you, as a student of Indian basketry, might want to pursue. For our purposes here, we have chosen a 100-year-old Yuki basket which contains a primary and a secondary band of joined rectangles in Red Bud, plus a number of rather ugly "splotches" which are often found in Yuki basketry. The Red Bud in the bands is very dark but displays all the characteristics of Red Bud pattern material.

The Yuki people live just north of the Pomos, several hundred miles, as the sea gull flies, north of San Francisco.

For purposes of this narrative, an assumption is made that the reader can identify Red Bud bark but does not recognize the other very old material. This basket was chosen as an example because the dark splotches, which are so typical of some Yuki baskets, prove what peeled Red Bud looks like, particularly in a very old basket.

The basket pictured in Figure 107 is a classic deep basin Yuki basket approximately 100 to 125 years old. The exact age is somewhat irrelevant; *it is simply old.* On first blush an observer may ask *"what the heck are those dark splotches?"* To a casual basketry student the splotches may be ugly, but to a dedicated basketry nut they are perhaps the best clues imaginable to confirm what 100-year-old peeled Red Bark looks like, and how it ages.

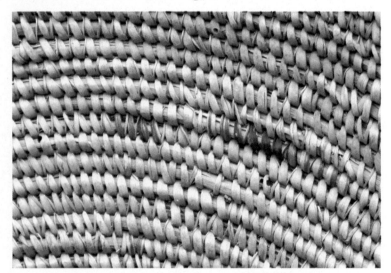

Figure 107. "Splotches" on an old Yuki basket, obtained from Bob Hickman of Old Sacramento.

In reading the literature, one finds that Yuki baskets have several traits which set them apart from those of their northern California neighbors: 1) they are about the only northwestern California people who coil clockwise (*right handed*), 2) they have a unique style of "start", 3) they use Red Bud more extensively than do their neighbors, and 4) they are often careless in stripping off the outer Red Bud bark.

By use of your trusty $4.98 (plus tax) magnifier, it doesn't take a *Phi Beta Kappa* to determine that the ugly dark splotches are actually fragments of Red Bud bark that were not properly stripped clean before the weaver strand was incorporated into the basket. If there is any question as to whether this material is, indeed, Red Bud bark, a good, close look at the dark material with your magnifier (see Figure 108) shows that the splotches have a few tiny white lenticels in the dark maroon-red bark. It is kind of amazing (to the author anyway) that American Indians discovered *lenticels* centuries before they discovered Willis Jepson. These *lenticels* are almost the signature of Red Bud bark!

Figure 108. Stitches showing carelessly removed
Red Bud Bark grading into cleanly peeled Red Bud.
Note the faint but tiny lenticels on the right end of the
splotch in the center-right, so typical of Red Bud Bark.

Next, take another good look at the ugly dark splotches, which you have just determined to be Red Bud bark, and notice that the Red Bud bark transitions into the sandy tan weaver strand, which you were trying to identify in the first place.

Now, even the author can figure out that if a weaver strand has Red Bud bark on parts of it, then the rest of that same weaver strand must also be Red Bud. You now have proven that the weathered tan weaver strand is actually peeled Red Bud. A close look will also show that the strand somewhat resembles peeled Willow, except perhaps a little more oily and perhaps with a tad more longitudinal striations. As a student of Indian basketry materials, you should store this image away firmly in the fleshy tablets of the memory.

Actually, there are a number of cases where simple deduction can prove a case as surely as in the above. For example, if a person determines that a given basket is relatively old and traditional, and that it has all the characteristics of a "Mission" basket, then a close look with a good magnifier will show that the reddish brown pattern material must be basal Juncus and cannot be Alder dyed Woodwardia fern stems, or "Sunburned Willow", or Yucca root. This logic may be negative logic but logic, none-the-less.

CHAPTER 6

GRAPHIC SUMMARY

A foregoing section, chapter three of this jumble of words, addressed some of the western American Indian tribes and a few of the plants they use(d) in creating their basketry. As stated repeatedly (at least several times anyway), this discussion is limited to only those Indian tribes in the western portions of North America, including Alaska and western Canada, that created a substantial amount of basketry. It is recognized that there are literally hundreds of Indian entities (tribes or bands) within the subject area which are not addressed herein. For example, California is reputed to have contained over 100 different tribal languages at the time of contact. If a language kind-of defines a tribe (which isn't exactly true) there must have been at least 100 tribes in California alone. However, because this treatise purports to deal only with Indian basketry and the plants used in their creation, only those tribes represented by at least a modicum of Indian baskets in either private or public collections, are addressed. In other words, if a tribe did not produce at least a few baskets for posterity, then that tribe is not addressed herein.

If California has a great amount of tribal diversity (over 100 languages), just image how many tribes there are in New Mexico, Arizona, Nevada, Oregon, Washington, Idaho, British Columbia, and Alaska. If there are that many tribes, and if this treatise were to include them all, then just imagine how long it would take for the printer to produce all the pages necessary to describe each and every one. Hopefully, omission of many of the tribes will not offend any tribal members, collectors, students, or civil liberty unions.

In chapter two, thirty-seven plants are listed that are,

or were, used in one form or another in the creation of an Indian basket, either as a warp, a weft, a weaver strand, a foundation material, or for a "start". It was stated, quite emphatically, (*I hope*) that 1) this list only covers a small, but important number of plants that were used in traditional Indian basketry, 2) a specific plant species in one region is not always the same as the same species in another region, 3) a cornucopia of materials was available for basketry use, but tribal or family tradition limited usage to only a selected few, 4) a specific plant name varies with the region; e.g., "Cedar" is a different genera or species depending upon where you find it, and, 5) Yucca species or varieties vary widely albeit they all may be called "Yucca" herein.

Chapter three speaks to the plant materials used by each of the 57 tribes addressed herein, concerning basketry styles, and the method by which plants were used. Several tribes are mentioned but not addressed in any detail. Because the information in chapter three is so verbose, an attempt was made to reduce it into a condensed format, arrayed in tabular form, so that the reader can follow usage of each plant material over a specific geographical region.

Tables 1 and 2, representing that summary, are presented in a fold-out format and summarize the plants used by each tribe. Table 1 covers thirty-seven plant materials and thirty-two California tribes, while Table 2 covers the same thirty-seven plants but only those tribes in the USA's southwest and the Pacific Northwest, including western Canada and Alaska.

Just a few words about the tables. They show either a W, S, F, or RARE in the abscissa (row) opposite a tribal name and in the ordinate (column) representing a plant material. W implies the plant was used as either a Warp, a Weft, or a Weaver strand by the appropriate tribe. S indicates the plant was used in the "Start", a F means the material was used in the plant's Foundation, and RARE suggests that the plant was used only rarely by the specific tribe.

A casual glance at the tables shows a scattering of Ws and Fs that may or may not make a lot of sense. However, in the cold light of morning, the author likes to say "the scatters the thing!" If the column shows a rather tight grouping of Ws or Fs, the reader should look to see if that grouping is defining a geographical range of that plant's usage. For example, Table 1, column 12, shows thirteen tribes using Deer Grass, all of which tribes are found in the southern Sierra Nevada Range or in southern California, which suggests that if a basket is found with Deer Grass as a foundation material, then it must have originated in the southern Sierras or south of the Tehachapi Mountain range.

Quite frequently, hybridization of weaving techniques involves using plants not normally used by the specific tribe; e.g., Juanita Nejo (Lopez), a famous basket maker on the Pechanga reservation in Riverside County, California, was born an Ipai (Northern Diegueno), not a Pechanga member. She learned to weave using Pine Needles in her early life as an Ipai member, but married a Pechanga (Luiseno) man and lived her married life on the Pechanga reservation and was widely known as a Pechanga lady. However, she continued to gather her Pine Needles in Ipai country and to weave in an Ipai style. This is a common trait in the Coachella Valley where intermarriage caused a hybridization of Cahuilla and Arizona basketry.

Likewise, negative use can be made of this table, For example, if Juncus appears in a basket along with Hazel, the red flag is up immediately because rarely, if ever, will these materials be used together. When you, the reader, discover such an anomaly, you may do well to reconsider your identification of either the Juncus or the Hazel.

True, the information on the tables is not all-inclusive, but it will at least aid in understanding a bit about what plant materials were used, when, and where.

BIBLIOGRAPHY
and
SUGGESTED READING

Abel-Vidor, Suzanne, Dot Brovarney, and Susan Billy
  1996: *Remember Your Relations, The Elsie Allen Baskets Family and Friends.* Grace Hudson Museum, Oakland Museum of California/Heyday Press, Berkeley, Calif.

Allen, Elsie
  1972: *Pomo Basketmaking, A supreme Art For the Weaver.* Naturegraph Publishers, Inc., Happy Camp, California.

Amsden, Charles
  n.d.: *The Ancient Basketmakers.* Number 11, Southwest Museum leaflets.

Anderson, Eugene N. Jr.
  1968: *The Chumash Indians of Southern California.*

Anderson, M. Kat,
  1996: *Ethnobotany of Deer Grass, Its uses and Fire Management by California Indian Tribes. in Economic Botany.*
  1996: *Tending the Wild,* in Restoration & Management Notes.
  2005: *Tending the Wild.* University of California Press, Berkeley, California.
  n.d.: *California Indian Horticulture.* unpublished ms.

Baird, Genevieve
  1976: *Northwest Indian Basketry.* Published to commemorate Washington State American Revolution.

Balls, Edward K.
  1962: *Early Uses of California Plants. A California Natural History Guide* # 10 series. University of California Press, Berkeley, California.

Barker, James M.
  1995: *Four Hands Weaving, Basketry of San Diego's*

Indigenous people. An exhibit catalogue by Palomar College's Boehm Gallery, San Marcos, California.

Barona Cultural Center
2004:   *Legacy from Our Mothers, Indian Basketry of San Diego County.* A catalogue of a Barona Museum event, Barona, California.

Barrett, Samuel A
1996:   *Pomo Indian Basketry.* Phoebe Hearst Museum of Anthropology, University of California, Berkeley.

Barrett, S.A. and E.W. Gifford
1933:   *Miwok Material Culture: Indian Life in the Yosemite Region.* A reprint of a publication by Yosemite Natural History Associates Inc. Yosemite National Park, Calif.

Basso, Keith H.
1970:   *The Cibecue Apache. Case studies in Cultural Anthropology,* Stanford University, Holt, Reinhart and Winston Publishers, Various cities.

Bates, Craig, and Martha J. Lee
1990:   *Traditions and Innovations, A history of Indians in the Yosemite-Mono Lake Region.* Yosemite Association, Yosemite National Park, California.

Bean, Lowell John, and Thomas Blackburn
1976:   *California Natives, A Theoretic Prospective.* Ballena Press, Ramona, California.

Bean, Lowell John, and Katherine Siva Saubel
1992:   *Temalpakh Cahuilla Indian Knowledge and Usage of Plants.* Malki Press, Morongo Indian Reservation, Banning, California.

Beauchamp, R. Mitchel
1986:   *Floral of San Diego County, California.* Sweetwater River Press, National City, California.

Bell, Maureen
1962:   *Karuk, The Upriver People.* Naturegraph Publishers Inc. Happy Camp, California.

Bernstein, Bruce
2003:   *The Language of Native American Baskets from the Weaver's View.* Smithsonian/The National Museum of the American Indian publishers, Washington D.C.
2005:   *The Ella Cain Collection of Mono Lake Paiute Basketry.*

Bibby, Brian,
   1996:   *The Fine Art of California Indian Basketry.* Crocker Art
           Museum, Sacramento, in conjunction with Heyday
           Press, Berkeley, California.
   2004:   *Precious Cargo, California Indian Cradles and
           Birthright Traditions.* Heyday Press publishers,
           Berkeley, California.

Bingaman, John W.
   1966:   *The Awahneechees, A Story of Yosemite Indians.* End-
           Kian Publishing Company, Lodi, California.

Brockman, C. Frank
   n.d.:   *Trees of North America.* No publisher or date

Brooks, Mary, and Jim Lowery
   2002:   *Plant Uses. a class syllabus.* Earth Skills, Frazier
           Park, California (self published.)

Brown, Alton K.
   1973:   *Indians of San Mateo County. in LA Peninsula.* Journal
           of San Mateo County Historical Association.

Brown, Vinson and Douglas Andrews
   1969:   *The Pomo Indians of California.* vol. 1 American Indian
           Map-Book Series. Naturegraph Publishers, Happy
           Camp, California.

Brusa, Betty War
   1975:   *Salinan Indians of California and their Neighbors.*
           Naturegraph Publishers, Happy Camp, California.

Burckhalter, David
   1982:   *Power of Seri Baskets.* in American West Mag, Jan.-
           Feb. 1982, pp 38-45.

Busby, Sharon,
   2003:   *Spruce Root Basketry of the Haida and Tlingit.*
           Marquand Books Inc. Seattle, and University of
           Washington Press,

Cain: William, and Art Silva
   n.d.:   Class syllabus University of California-Irvine.

California Indian Arts Association, Video Series
   1994:   Dr. Moser and Bill Cain, *Cahuilla Basket Weavers.*
   1994:   Justin Farmer, *Diegueno Baskets.*
   1995:   Jan Timbrook, *Chumash Baskets and Culture.*
   1996:   Elizabeth Villas, *Steffa Baskets at Pomona College.*
   1996:   Dr. Moser and Justin Farmer, *Rattlesnake baskets.*

1996: Jeff Rigby, *Chumash Cave Baskets.*
1997: Bill Cain, *Indian Basketry Hats.*
1997: Southwest Museum, *The Indian Basketry Collection.*
1998: Chris Roman, *An Open Twined Basket.*

Campbell, Elizabeth Crozer
1931: *An Archaeological Survey of the Twenty Nine Palms Region.* A Southwest Museum Paper Number seven, reprint of 1963.

Campbell, Paul
1998: *Twined Double Basket Pomo Fish Trap.* an unpublished ms.

Casebeer, Maryruth
2004: *Discovering California Shrubs.* Hooker Press, Sonora, California.

Chase, Don M., Carl Purde, and Clara MacNaughton
1977: *Basket-Maker Artists.* Self published, Sebastopol, California. CIBA (California Indian Basketmakers Association)
2002: *A Resource Directory*

Conner, J. Torrey
1896: *Confessions of a Basket Collector,* in *LAND OF SUNSHINE* vol. V/3 May 1896.

Cuero, Ted, and Margaret Langton
2002: *Lets Talk I'ipay AA.* An Introduction to the Mesa Grande Diegueno (Ipai) Language.

Dakin, Susanna Bryant
1939: *A Scotch Paisano in Old Los Angeles.* Hugo Reid's Life in California 1832-1852. a 1978 reprint.

Dalrymple, Larry
1982: *Contemporary American Indian Basketry.* Self Published, Modesto, California.
2000: *Indian Basketmakers of California and the Great Basin.* Museum of New Mexico Press, Santa Fe, N.M.

Dale, Nancy
1985: *Flowering Plants, The Santa Monica Mountain, Coastal & Chaparral Regions of Southern California.* Capra Press in cooperation with the California Native Plant Society.

Daly, Julie
2000: *Woven History, Native American Basketry.* Collection

of the Clark County Historical Museum, Vancouver, Washington.

Davidson, Anstruther, M.D. and George L Moxley
1923: *Flora of Southern California.* Times-Mirror Press, Los Angeles, California.

Davis, Edward H
1931: *The Pursuits of a Museum Collector.* in "Touring Topics" magazine, (Auto Club of So. Cal.)

Davis, E.L and William Allen
1967: *Diegueno Coiled Baskets in San Diego Museum of Man.* Ethnic Technology notes No 1, San Diego Museum of Man, California.

Dawson, Lawrence and James Deetz
1965: *A Corpus of Chumash Basketry.* Annual Report, Archaeology Survey, Department of Anthropology, University of California, Los Angeles.

Dean, Sharon E., et al
2004: *Weaving a Legacy: Indian Baskets & the People of Owens Valley, California.* University of Utah Press, Salt Lake City, Utah.

Densmore, Frances
1928: *How Indians Used Wild Plant For Food, Medicine & Crafts.* A 1974 reissue by Dover Press, New York.

Dittemore, Diane D, and Mary Odegard
1998: *Eccentric Marks on Western Apache Coiled Basketry.* in American Indian Arts magazine vol. 23/2 Spring 1998.

Downs, James F.
1962: *The Two Worlds of the Washo, An Indian Tribe of California and Nevada.* Case Studies in Cultural Anthropology, Stanford University, Holt, Reinhart and Winston Inc.

Dozier, Edward P.
1966: *Hano, A Tewa Indian Community in Arizona.* Case studies in Anthropology publication, Stanford University, Holt, Reinhart and Winston publishers, various cities.

Duff, Wilson
1965: *The Indian History of British Columbia.* British Columbia Provincial Museum. volume 1, The Impact

of the White Man, Province Of British Columbia, Ministry of the Provincial Secretary.

Dutton, Bertha
n.d.:   *The Rancheria, Utes, and Southern Paiute People.*
Prentice-Hall Inc.

Elsasser, A.B.
1962:   *Indians of Sequoia and Kings Canyon National Park.*
A 1972 edition of the Sequoia Natural History Association, Three Rivers, California.

Epple, Anne Orth
1995:   *Field Guide to the Plants of Arizona.* Globe Pequot
Press Guilford, Connecticut.

Euler, Robert C.
1979:   *The Havasupai of the Grand Canyon.* In American
West Magazine XV1/3. 1979 pp 12-17.

Evens, Glen L and T.N. Campbell
1970:   *Indian Baskets of the Paul Seashore Collection.* Texas
Memorial Museum, Museum notes No. 11

Evans, Mike
2007:   Personal contact

Farmer, Justin F.
1991:   *Indian Basketry Material Preparation.* Self published,
Fullerton, California.
1993:   *California Indian Baskets: Their Characteristics and
Materials Used.* Self published, Fullerton, California
2004:   *Southern California Luiseno Indian Baskets.* Justin
Farmer Foundation Publishers, Fullerton, California.
2006:   *Creation of a Southern California "Mission" Basket.* Self
published, Fullerton, California.

Field, Clark
1964:   *Arts and Romance of Indian Basketry.* A nation-wide
cursory discussion of cradles and basketry. Published
by Philbrook Art Center, Tulsa, Oklahoma.

Fifield, Terence
1995:   *Thorne River Basket: Description Context and
Opportunity.* an unpublished paper

Fitzgerald, Sallie
1911:   *Priscilla Basketry Book*

Fitzhugh, William W. and Aron Crowell
   1988: *Crossroads of Continents, Culture of Siberia and
          Alaska.* Smithsonian Institute, Washington D.C.

Frey, Winfred
   1904: *Humboldt Indians.* In OUT WEST magazine, vol. XXI/6
          Dec 1904.

Fulkerson, Mary Lee
   1995: *Weavers of Tradition & Beauty, Basketmakers of
          the Great Basin.* University of Nevada Press, Reno,
          Nevada.

Gasser, Maria del Carmen
   1996: *"My Dear Miss Nicholson".* Letters and Myths by
          William R. Benson, a Pomo Indian. Published by the
          editor.

Geiger, Maynard OFM PhD.
   1960: *Indians of Santa Barbara in Paganism and
          Christianity.*

Godfrey, Elizabeth
   1941: *Yosemite Indians.* A 1973 revised edition of Yosemite
          Natural History Association Inc. Yosemite National
          Park, California, vol. XX No. 7.

Gogol, John M.
   1985: *Cowlitz Indian Basketry.* In American Indian Basketry
          magazine vol. v. # 20 , pp 4-20.

Goodrich, Jennie, Claudia Lawson, and Vana Parrish Lawson
   1980: *Kashaya Pomo Plants.* Heyday Books, Berkeley,
          California.

Grimes, John R., Christian F. Feest, and Mary Lou Curran
   2002: *Uncommon Legacies*: Native American Art from the
          Peabody Essex Museum. University of Washington
          Press.

Gunther, Erna
   1945/73: *Ethnobotany of Western Washington.* University of
          Washington Press, Seattle and London.

Hall, Sharlot M.
   1907: *Indians of Arizona.* In OUT WEST magazine vol.
          XXVII/6 Dec. 1907.

Hass, Jim
    2005:   *The Ella M. Cain Collection of Mono Lake Paiute Basketry.* Bonham & Butterfield (see also Bruce Bernstein).

Hedges Ken
    Var.: Personal contact
    1997:   *Fibers and Forms: Native American Basketry of the West.* San Diego Museum of Man, San Diego, California.

Heizer, Robert F.
    1966:   *Languages, Territories and Names of California Indian Tribes.* University of California Press, Berkeley and Los Angeles, California.

Heizer, Robert F. (editor), Smithsonian Institution
    1974:   *The Costanoan Indians.* Local History Studies vol. 18, California History Center, De Anza College, Cupertino, California.
    1978:   *Handbook of North American Indians.* volume 8, California. Smithsonian Institution, contains 54 authors, all on California Indian basketry and culture.

Hendryx, Michael
    1991:   *Plants and the People: Ethnobotany of the Karuk Tribe.* Siskiyou County Museum, Yreka, California.
    2006-8: Personal contact

Hickman, Bob (Gallery of the American West-Old Sacramento)
    Var.:   Personal Contact

Hickman, James
    1996:   *Jepson Manual, Higher Plants of California.* A revision of Jepson's 1923 handbook, University of California Press, Berkeley and Los Angeles, California.

Hogue, Helen
    1977:   *Wintu Trails.* Shasta Historical Society, Redding, California.

Hoveman, Alice
    2002:   *Journal of Justice, the Wintun People and the Salmon.* Turtle Bay Exploration Park, Redding, California.

Howe, Carrol B.
    1968:   *Ancient Tribes of the Klamath Country.* Binford and Mort, Publishers, Portland, Oregon.

Hudson, Travis, and Thomas C. Blackburn
    1979:   *Material Culture of the Chumash Interaction Sphere.*
           vol. 1, Food Procurement and Transportation. Ballena
           Press & Santa Barbara Natural History Cooperative
           Publication.
    1981:   same. vol. 2.

Hungry Wolf, Adolf and Beverly
    1989:   *Indian Tribes of The Northern Rockies.* Book Publishing
           Company, Summertown, TN.

James, Cheewa
    2008:   *Modoc, The tribe that wouldn't Die.* Naturegraph
           Publishers, Happy Camp, California.

James, George Wharton
    1903:   *Indian Basketry & How to Make Baskets.* A 1970
           reprint of James' original work, by Rio Grande Press
           Inc. Glorieta, New Mexico.

Jepson, Willis Linn
    1923:   *Manual of Flowering Plants of California.* California
           School Book Depository.

Jolley, Ginger
    1985:   *How to Weave a Pine Needle Basket.* Privately
           published. Lake Arrowhead, California.

Jones, Joan Megan PhD.
    1982:   *Art and Style of Western Indian Basketry.* Maryhill
           Collection. Hancock House Publishers, Blaine,
           Washington.

Kelley, Isabel T.
    1930:   *Yuki Basketry.* A reprint of a U.C. Berkeley
           Publication, University of California Press, Berkeley,
           California.

Kern County Museum
    n.d.:   *Yokuts Basketry.* An unpublished monograph, author
           not stated.

Knudtson, Peter M.
    1977:   *The Wintun Indians of California.* Naturegraph
           Publishers, Inc. Happy Camp, California.

Kozloff, Eugene
    1976:   *Plants and Animals of the Pacific Northwest.* Greystone
           Books, Vancouver/Toronto- University of Washington
           Press, Seattle, Washington.

Kroeber, A. L.
  1908: *Ethnography of the Cahuilla Indians.* University
         of California Publication American Archaeology &
         Ethnology, vol. 8, No. 2.
  1907: *Handbook of the Indians of California.* A Dover reprint
  1926: *Basketry Designs of the Mission Indians.* Guide Leaflet
         Series No. 55, second edition, American Museum of
         Natural History, New York, New York.

Landberg, Leif C.W.
  1965: *The Chumash Indians of Southern California.*
         Southwest Museum Papers Number Nineteen

Lang, Carol E.
  2000: *Natural Materials for Basketmaking.* Self published

Lang, Kathleen Ward
  1993: *Devil's Claw and Catspaws: A thread into the past.* A
         masters thesis, unpublished.

Latta, Frank F.
  1977: *Handbook of the Yokuts Indians.* A 1977 reprint of the
         1949 edition, Bear State Books, Santa Cruz, Calif.

Lee, Molly
  1994: *Alaskan Eskimo Coiled Basketry.* In American Indian
         Arts magazine vol. 20/4, autumn 1994.

Lopez, Raul: (see Moser)

MacNaughton, Clara
  1903: *Nevada Indian Baskets and Their Makers.* OUT WEST
         magazine vol. XVIII/4, April 1903, and XVIII/5, May
         1903.

Marr, Carolyn
  1991: No title. in American Indian Arts Mag. 16/2 Spring
         1991.

Massachusetts Council of the Arts and Humanities
  1975: *American Indian Basketry Work.* The George Walter
         Vincent Smith Art Museum, Springfield Mass.

Mathewson, Margaret ("Peg")
  n.d.: *Ancient Art and Technologies.* An unpublished
         monograph.
  n.d.: *Contemporary California Basketry Fiber Plants.*
         unpublished.

McGreevy, Susan Brown
   1999:   *Design Development in Navajo Baskets in America*. In
           Indian Arts magazine vol. 24/3 Summer 1999.

Merrill, Ruth Earl
   1980:   *Plants Used in Basketry by the California Indians*. A
           reprint by Acoma Books, Ramona, California.

Miles, Charles
   1963:   *Indian and Eskimo Artifacts of North America*. Bonanza
           Books, New York, MXMLXIII.

Miller, Sheryl F.
   1989:   *Hopi Basketry*. In American Indian Arts mag. 15/1
           Winter.
   1999:   *Designs in Hopi Baskets*. In American Indian Arts
           magazine.

Moerman, Daniel E.
   1998:   *Native American Ethnobotany*. The Timber press,
           Portland, Oregon.

Moser, Christopher L, PhD
   1981:   *Rods, Bundles, and Stitches* (with Raul Lopez).
           Riverside Museum Press, Riverside, California.
   1986:   *Native American Basketry of Central California*.
           Riverside Museum Press, Riverside, California.
   1989:   *American Indian Basketry of Northern California*.
           Riverside Museum Press, Riverside, California.
   1993:   *Native American Basketry of Southern California*.
           Riverside Museum Press, Riverside, California,

Mozingo, Hugh N.
   1987:   *Shrubs of the Great Basin*. University of Nevada Press,
           Reno, Nevada.

National Audubon Society
   1986:   Familiar Trees of North America - West. A 2004
           edition, Alfred A. Knopf Publication, New York, New
           York.

Navajo School of Indian Basketry
   1903:   *Indian Basket Weaving*. A 1971 reprint by Dover
           Publications Inc., New York, New York.

Nevada State Museum: (see Tuohy)

Noble D.D.,W.B.
   1904:   *A Day with the Mono Indians*. OUT WEST magazine,
           vol. XX/5, May 1904.

O'Neale, Lila M.
    1932: *Yurok-Karok Basket Weavers*. Phoebe Hearst Museum
        of Anthropology, a 1995 University of California
        reprint.

Ortiz, Alfonso (editor), Smithsonian Institution
    1979: *Handbook of North American Indians* Volume 9,
        Southwest.
    1983: *Handbook of North American Indians* Volume 10,
        Southwest.

Porter, Frank W.
    1988: *Native American Basketry*. An Annotated Bibliography

Potts, Marie
    1977: *The Northern Maidu*. Naturegraph Publishers Inc.
        Happy Camp, California.

Preston, Richard J Jr.
    1946: *North American Trees*. The MIT Press (Massachusetts
        Institute of Technology) Cambridge, Mass.

Puffer, Herb
    Var.: Personal contact

Purdy, Carl
    1901: *Pomo Indian Baskets*. "Out West" Magazine, December
        1901, and January, February, and March, 1902 vols.
        XVI-1,2,&3.

Rancho Santa Ana Botanical Gardens
    1988: *The Basketry Trail, A trail guide to plants in the
        gardens*. Rancho Santa Ana Botanical Gardens,
        Claremont, California.

Rawls, James J
    1984: *Indians of California, The Changing Image*. University
        of Oklahoma Press, Norman, Oklahoma and London,
        England.

Reece, Verna
    Var.: Personal contact

Renfro, Elizabeth
    1992: *The Shasta Indians of California and Their Neighbors*.
        Naturegraph Publishers, Inc. Happy Camp, California.

Rigby Jeffrey Walter
    1987: *Detecting Cultural and Linguistic Differences in
        the Southern Chumash Interaction Sphere*. An
        unpublished thesis from UCLA.

Roberts, Helen H.
   1929:   *Basketry of the San Carlos Apache Indians.*1972
           reprint volume XXXI Part II, Rio Grande Press, Inc.

Rothtelki, Gloria
   1979:   *Collecting Traditional American Basketry.* E.P. Button,
           New York, New York.

Schaaf, Gregory
   2006:   *American Indian Baskets* I. American Indian Art Series
           volume six. a 1500 Artist bibliography, CIC Press,
           Santa Fe, N.M.

Schlick, Mary D.
   n.d: *Wasco Wishram Basketry.* In American Indian
           Basketry, vol. 4 No. 20 pages 21-27.
   1991:   No Title. in American Indian Arts mag. 16/3 Summer
           1991.

Schlick, Mary Dodds
   1994:   *Columbia River Basketry, Gifts of the Ancestors, Gifts
           of the Earth.* University of Washington Press, Seattle,
           Washington.

Schultz, Paul E.
   1954:   *Indians of Lassen Volcanic National Park and Vicinity.*
           Loomis Museum Associates, Lassen Volcanic National
           Park, Mineral, California.

Schwantes, Carlos Arnaldo
   1989:   *The Pacific Northwest, an Interpretive History.*

Silva, Arthur M and William C Cain
   1976:   *California Indian Basketry: An Artistic Overview.* An
           exhibit catalogue of the Cypress College of Fine Arts,
           Cypress, California.

Slater, Eva
   2000: *Panamint-Shoshone Basketry.* Sagebrush Press,
           Morongo Valley, California.

Smith, Gerald PhD
   1977:   *The Mojaves, Historic Indians of San Bernardino
           County.*

Smith, Gerald PhD, and Ruth Dee Simpson
   1964:   *Indian Basket Makers of San Bernardino County.* San
           Bernardino County Museum, California.

Smith, Sarah Bixby
　　1925:　*Adobe Days*. 1972 reprint, Valley Publishers, Fresno,
　　　　　　California.

Smithsonian, (see also Ortiz, Alfonso and Heizer, Robert F.)
　　　　　　Handbook of North American Indians. Various
　　　　　　volumes, Washington, D.C.
　　1990:　Volume 7, Northwest
　　1978:　Volume 8, California
　　1979:　Volume 9, Southwest
　　1981:　Volume10, Southwest
　　1986:　Volume 11, Great Basin
　　1998:　Volume 12, Plateau
　　2001:　Volume 13, Plains (2 volumes)

Stribling, Mary Lou
　　1974:　*Crafts From North American Indian Arts*. Crown
　　　　　　Publishers, Inc. New York, New York.

Sweet, Muriel
　　1976:　*Common Edible and Useful Plants of the West*.
　　　　　　Naturegraph Publishers Inc. Happy Camp, California.

Tanner, Clara Lee
　　1976:　*Prehistoric Southwestern Craft Art*.

Timbrook, Jan
　　2007:　*Chumash Ethnobotany*. Santa Barbara Museum of
　　　　　　Natural History, Santa Barbara, and Heyday Press
　　　　　　Berkley, California.

Tuohy, Donald R. and Doris L Randy, Eds.
　　1974:　Collection of papers on Aboriginal baskets. Nevada
　　　　　　State Museum, Anthropological Paper Number 16,
　　　　　　Carson City, Nevada.

Turnbaugh, Sarah Peabody and William Turnbaugh
　　1986:　*Indian Baskets*. Schiffer Publishing Ltd., West
　　　　　　Chester, Pennsylvania.

Underhill, Ruth PhD
　　1941:　*The Northern Paiute Indians of California and Nevada*.
　　　　　　US Bureau of Indian Affairs , Washington, D.C. U.S.
　　　　　　Department of Commerce.
　　1944:　*Indians of the Pacific Northwest*. Published by the
　　　　　　Branch of Education, Bureau of Indian Affairs,
　　　　　　Washington, D.C.　　U.S. Department of Commerce.
　　n.d.:　*Federal and State Indian Reservations and Indian
　　　　　　Trust Areas*.

n.d.:   *Indians of Southern California.* Sherman Pamphlets number 2, US Bureau of Indian Affairs, Washington, D.C. U.S. Department of Commerce.

Wheat, Margaret M.
  1967:   *Survival Arts of the Primitive Paiutes.* University of Nevada Press, Reno, Nevada.

Wilson, B.D.
  1852:   *Indians of Southern California in 1852.* University of Nebraska Press, Lincoln and London reprint of 1995

Winther, Barbara
  2000:   *Yuki and Yuki Style Basketry.* In American Indian Arts magazine, Summer, 2000.
  1996:   *Visiting Four Pomo Baskets.* In American Indian Art magazines vol. 21/4 Autumn 1996.

NOTES